Karen Leigh Da...

# Mixed–
# Breed Cats

Everything about Purchase, Care,
Nutrition, Health Care, Behavior,
and Showing

Filled with Full-color Photographs

Illustrations by
Tana Hakanson Monsalve

D0922567

BARRON'S

# 2 CONTENTS

# HISTORY AND DESCRIPTION OF THE MIXED BREED

## By Any Other Name

You want a cat but can't decide between a Siamese, a Somali, or a Singapura? A Manx or a Maine Coon? A Birman or a British Shorthair? How about a mixture of each? Whether you call it simply a household pet, a non-pedigreed cat, a stray, an alley cat, an American domestic, or, as the British say, a *moggy,* the mixed-breed cat is still a cat like any other. Plus, the mixed breed has the advantage of being the most prevalent type of cat available in most parts of the world today.

Charming and intelligent, mixed-breed cats have been the companions of humans for centuries, long before feline enthusiasts began to selectively breed and develop purebred bloodlines. A *purebred* cat, of course, is bred from members of a recognized breed and has a recorded ancestry. A non-pedigreed, *mixed-breed* cat, on the other hand, is generally understood to be the feline equivalent of what canine enthusiasts affectionately refer to as a mutt. While sometimes it may be obvious that one parent was of a specific breed—such as a

*Many cat shows have Household Pet classes that allow mixed-breed, non-purebred cats, like this part Abyssinian, to be shown.*

Siamese—the mixed-breed cat's ancestry is, in most cases, unknown and unverifiable.

Today, the more politically correct and probably the more accurate term for cats of uncertain ancestry is *random bred.* Language purists may argue that the term mixed breed more properly means that at least two recognized breeds have been mixed or *crossbred*—for instance, a Persian was mated with an American Shorthair, or a Russian Blue was crossed with an Abyssinian to produce offspring. Yet, the more common reference—*mixed breed*—remains well understood by the general populace to mean a little bit of this and a little dash of that, with who knows what else added for extra flair. For this reason, we will stick with the common usage—mixed-breed cats—in this book.

## Origins and Domestication

Whether you choose to call them mixed-breed or random-bred cats, all cats, whether mixed or purebreds, descended from a few wild progenitors. In fact, most experts agree that the modern domestic cat, *Felis catus,* likely descends from a shorthaired wildcat, called *Felis lybica,* that roamed the plains of ancient Africa and western Asia. Today's tabbies still retain the distinctive striped markings and the lithe, muscular body of this wild ancestor.

Unlike most wild animals, *Felis lybica* often chose to live near human settlements and hunt the vermin that would inevitably seek out and raid the food stores. As a result, the cat gradually accepted domestication as a reasonable trade-off for the privilege of staying close to an easy and stable food source. However, the cat was one of the last of our modern-day animals to be domesticated, lagging far behind the dog, who became man's hunting companion some 16,000 years ago.

History generally credits the Egyptians with being among the first people to domesticate the cat, approximately 3,500 to 5,000 years ago. Astute agriculturists, the Egyptians most certainly recognized the cat's inestimable value in protecting their grain stores from rats and mice. One might imagine that the Egyptians began enticing these prowling wild felines to stay close to their settlements, perhaps by leaving scraps of food near their grain stores. As a result, taming or *domestication* of wild cats gradually took place. So valuable was their natural pest-control service that cats enjoyed an extended period of elevated status during this early era of human civilization. In fact, archaeological discoveries suggest that Egyptians worshipped cats as representatives of household gods. The Egyptian goddess Bast was often depicted as a woman with a cat's head. So revered were these animals that symbolized their religious beliefs that Egyptians mourned the loss when a cat died, and even mummified the animal's remains for entry into the afterlife. As one may guess, the penalty for killing a cat in those days was death.

Supporting the theory of Egyptian domestication and African origins is the fact that many of today's shorthaired cats remarkably resemble the stately Egyptian cats depicted in ancient paintings and sculptures. Likewise, some of their longhaired cousins, with their tufted ears and cheeks, retain the Lynx-like look of their wild, African ancestor, *Felis lybica*.

# From Gods to Devils

Not all cultures worshipped cats as gods the way the Egyptians did. By the Middle Ages, cats had spread to European nations, transported there no doubt by traders who, realizing their worth, carried specimens back to their homelands for rodent control. The thirteenth century proved to be a bleak time for cats. Along with their human associates accused of witchcraft by the Christian church, cats became symbols of evil, devil worship, and pagan practices. As a result, they were persecuted, tortured, burned, and killed in the cruelest ways.

In one of the subtle ironies of history, however, retribution for this unjust sentencing came swiftly in the form of the Black Death, which fell upon western Europe in the mid-1300s and, within approximately four years, wiped out nearly half of the human population there. The Black Death was the bubonic plague, a deadly infection spread by disease-bearing rodents and the fleas that live off of their blood. The bite of an infected flea transmitted the disease from rat to man.

In retrospect, historians have suggested that the deliberate and systematic elimination of cats from the unsanitary streets and crowded towns of Europe during this time may have contributed to the rapid spread of bubonic plague. Unaware of the relationship between rats, fleas, and the plague, people caught up in the misguided religious and political fervor of the time effectively reduced the cat population that was helping to keep the rodents under control. In exercising this serious error in judgment, they may have unwittingly helped tip the odds in favor of a devastating epidemic.

In time, the Black Death ran its course, but not without incurring profound social changes that would signal the end of the Middle Ages. The persecution of cats eventually ended as well, as people once again came to appreciate their role in reducing rodent populations. At the dawn of a modern age, the domestic cat emerged from one of the darkest chapters in world history to begin a new journey into the heart of humankind.

## True Pioneers

While we know that domestic cats were in Europe by the Middle Ages, no one knows for sure exactly when they first arrived in the New World. Cats may have crossed the ocean as early as the Vikings or Columbus, but by the 1600s, they were most certainly coming along for the ride with European immigrants aboard sailing ships. The breed lore of the American Shorthair cat even mentions the *Mayflower* as one possible mode of transport. Such a tale is not implausible, since cats were brought along on long sea voyages in those days to hunt the rats and mice that ate the ship's food supplies. Owing to this practice, North America's domestic cats likely are descendants of cats brought from the British Isles and other western European countries.

Upon arrival in the New World, the cats were released and likely extended their pest-control duties in and around the new farms and colonies being settled. For centuries, these working mousers flourished in the fields and barns of America's pioneers, allowing natural selection to mold them and multiplying into a durable, diversified lot.

By the late 1800s, people had begun to view cats as more than mere mousers. As cat shows and the *cat fancy*—the collective term used to describe those interested in breeding and showing purebred cats—developed first in England, then spread to America, cats gained popularity as companion animals. People even began importing exotic breeds, such as longhaired and Siamese cats, from abroad. Some of these cats were allowed to run free and mingle with the domestic shorthair stock already flourishing on native soil. As a result, kittens began to crop up with varying coat lengths, color patterns, and temperaments, lending even more diversity to the melting pot.

## How Cat Shows Started

Harrison Weir staged the first cat show in 1871 at London's Crystal Palace. Weir also developed the first breed standards by which cats were judged in those days and served as president of Great Britain's first national cat club, which issued the first feline stud book in the late 1800s.

The United States was quick to follow Great Britain's lead, as cat exhibits and judgings have taken place here since the 1870s, but an official all-breed show held in 1895 at New York's Madison Square Garden marked the actual beginning of interest among North American cat fanciers. In 1899 the first and oldest U.S. registry, the American Cat Association (ACA), was formed to keep records.

Today, several other cat-registering associations exist in North America. They include the Cat Fanciers' Association (CFA), the American Cat Fanciers' Association (ACFA), the International Cat Association (TICA), the Cat Fanciers' Federation (CFF), the American Association of

*(above) Litters of random-bred kittens are readily available for adoption every spring.*

*(below) A calico cat is not a breed but a color best described as intermingling patches of white, black, and red.*

Cat Enthusiasts (AACE), the National Cat Fanciers' Association (NCFA), the United Feline Organization (UFO), the Canadian Cat Association (CCA), and the Traditional Cat Association (TCA). Each association has its own show rules and breed standards, but all maintain stud books, register purebred cats, and verify pedigrees. Most of them also charter clubs, sanction shows, and present awards and titles.

While preference is given to purebred cats in the cat show world, most associations sponsor household pet (HHP) categories in which mixed-breed cats and kittens can compete and earn awards (see page 89 for information about showing household pets). HHP classes existed as early as the mid-1960s, but they were primarily "sideshows" to the purebred

*Cats have not been domesticated as long as dogs have.*

*Today's tabbies still retain the distinctive striped markings of their wild ancestors.*

competition, judged by a local disc jockey or someone other than a qualified judge. Often, the so-called "judge" considered it more fun

to choose the meanest, fattest, or strangest-looking cat, a practice that actually demeaned the mixed-breed cat. The Happy Household Pet Cat Club, founded in 1968, and a group of its exhibitors from the Sacramento, California, area were instrumental in changing this by lobbying for fairer standards and equality in judging for HHPs. As a result, TICA was the first association to license HHP specialty judges.

Today, the awards and show procedures for HHP competition are more in line with pure-bred competition. TICA, ACFA, CFF, AACE, UFO, and TCA also maintain registries for non-pedigreed household pets. To show your household pet, you usually must register the cat with the association sanctioning the event. The association uses the registration information to score and track awards. The world's largest association, CFA, does *not* register non-purebreds, but many CFA-sponsored shows and clubs do have household pet categories that also award year-end honors to the top winners. The Happy Household Pet Cat Club, an international organization open to all feline fanciers, also registers random-bred cats, which allows its members to submit cat show scores and claim titles.

## Long- and Shorthaired Cats

Today's domestic cats come in two basic coat lengths: long and short. The shorthaired variety is more common because the gene for a short coat is always dominant. This means that, to be born with short hair, a kitten has to inherit the gene for this trait from only one parent. The gene for a longhair coat is always recessive. To be born with long hair, a kitten must inherit a gene for this trait from *both* parents.

The kitten that inherits a shorthair gene from one parent and a longhair gene from the other will be a shorthaired cat, even though it carries a "hidden" longhair gene. Due to the dominance of the shorthair gene, the gene for long hair is not expressed; however, a short-haired cat that carries both types of genes is capable of producing either short- or long-haired offspring when paired with a mate carrying like genes.

## Forever Tabbies

While our modern-day domestic cats come in varying coat lengths, colors, and color patterns, they all are genetically *tabbies*, like their wild African ancestors. Most people recognize the tabby as a cat that has pronounced stripes and bars on its coat, tail, and legs, and frown marks that form an intricate "M" on the forehead. The *classic* or *blotched tabby* has wide stripes, swirls, or blotches, often forming a recognizable bull's-eye pattern on the sides. The more common *mackerel tabby* has thinner stripes running from the backbone down the sides resembling fish ribs, hence the name. There are also rare *spotted tabbies*, which, as the name implies, sport spots instead of stripes. And there are tabbies with no stripes at all.

The Abyssinian and Somali breeds represent a unique form of tabby without stripes called the *agouti* pattern. These two closely related breeds—one a shorthaired variety, the other a longhair—are noted for their reddish-brown hair "ticked" with bands of darker color. The ticking, or agouti pattern, results from alternating light- and dark-colored bands on each hair shaft, giving the coat a delicately flecked appearance. The pattern occurs in some other species as well, such as squirrels, and serves as excellent camouflage.

Of the tabby varieties, the most common colors are the red tabby (sometimes called orange, yellow, or ginger), which bears deep, rich red markings against a lighter red or yellow ground color; the silver or gray tabby, which sports black stripes against a silver or gray background; and the brown tabby, which has black markings on a reddish-brown background.

# Cats of Many Colors

If all cats are genetically tabbies, then how did we end up with the plethora of colors and patterns we see in domestic cats today? Over time, genetic mutations have occurred that, depending on how genes are arranged in a particular individual, may result in masking or suppressing the distinctive tabby markings. Yet, some variation of the tabby gene remains present in all cats. If a cat inherits genes that completely mask the stripes and bars, it will be a *self* or solid color, but underneath, it's still a tabby.

Generally speaking, dominant genes tend to produce darker, denser colors, such as black or red (also called orange), while recessive genes, in the right combination, will produce *dilute* colors that are paler than their dominant counterparts. For example, the color gray, which cat fanciers call *blue,* is the recessive or dilute form of black. Likewise, a cream-colored cat is a paler shade of dominant red.

There are also many patterns that produce interesting color combinations in cats. A common genetic occurrence referred to as the *white spotting factor* randomly applies splashes of white to the face, feet, and belly, or, in the case of the calico cat, draws dramatic white patches among intermingling blotches of black and orange. Interestingly, calicos and *tortoiseshells* (which have a patchwork of black and orange blotches like the calico, but without the white) are nearly always females. The lovely patchwork of black and orange is a sex-linked trait produced by genes carried on the female (XX) chromosomes.

The pointed pattern, characterized by darker points on the cat's face, tail, feet, and ears against a lighter body color, predictably appears in certain purebred cats, such as the Siamese, the Himalayan, and the Ragdoll.

Aside from solids, tabbies, and cats with points, there are also silvers, shadeds, smokes, particolors, and bicolors. Silvers, shadeds, and smokes have darker-tipped hairs lying against a paler ground color or undercoat color, which gives the coat a contrasting, shimmering effect, especially when the cat moves and the fur parts. *Particolor* is a broad term for a coat of two or more colors, such as a tortoiseshell. A *bicolor* cat has a coat of two colors, one of which is white. While many purebreds are bred specifically for their coloring, all of these beautiful colors, patterns, and markings can appear randomly in the mixed genetic bag that makes up our treasured stock of non-pedigreed, domestic cats.

# ACQUIRING YOUR MIXED BREED

## Mixed Breed vs. Purebred

Certainly, acquiring a purebred cat has some advantages. Purebreds have a recorded ancestry and certain inherited qualities that make their appearance and temperament more predictable. When you buy a purebred kitten, you can reasonably expect that it will grow up to look much like its parents and share similar behavioral traits. With a mixed-breed kitten, however, you can only guess as to how a particular individual may turn out as an adult.

Still, for the person who merely wants a cat for a companion and has no interest in being a professional breeder, there are several good reasons for acquiring a mixed-breed cat:

✔ Random-bred "alley" cats make just as good companions as purebred felines.

✔ Non-pedigreed cats are much less expensive to acquire than purebreds, although the cost of their care is the same.

✔ Non-pedigreed cats are generally more readily available for adoption, and thus easier to find and acquire, while certain breeds may have a waiting list for kittens.

✔ Because random-bred cats spring from a larger, more varied gene pool, the majority are generally quite hardy and healthy, and with proper nutrition and good veterinary care can live an average 15 to 20 years.

✔ By acquiring a mixed-breed animal, you may save a life by providing a home for a cat that otherwise might be destroyed for lack of one or die of neglect. Every year, millions of dogs and cats in animal shelters are humanely put to death simply because there aren't enough homes to go around for all of them.

As you consider getting a cat, remember that your new relationship could last at least a decade or longer. For greatest compatibility, the cat you select as your long-term friend must suit your personality and lifestyle. Before you commit, know what you want in a cat companion. To help you decide, consider the following:

## One Cat or Two?

If you can afford the feeding and medical expenses for more than one cat, consider getting two. Like people, cats can become bored and lonely when forced to stay alone all day while you are away at work. One way to avoid this problem is to get two kittens at the same time, preferably at about the same age, so they can bond as friends and keep each other company. Despite their aloof, solitary reputation, cats are highly social animals, and cat acquaintances clearly enjoy each other's companionship.

*This regal-looking gentleman is called a "tuxedo" cat because of the way his black coat is dressed up with distinctive white markings on the face, neck, belly, and paws.*

# Male or Female?

The sex of the cat you choose as your companion should not matter. Both males and females make equally fine companions.

How can you tell whether a kitten is a male or a female? Raise the tail and look at the rear end. In the female, the genital opening looks like a small slit and appears directly below the anus. In the male, the anus and penis are spaced farther apart, and both openings are round.

# Spaying and Neutering

You definitely will want to spay or neuter your cat when it reaches the appropriate age. Veterinarians traditionally recommend that males be neutered between eight and ten months of age and that females be spayed at six months, but the surgery can now be performed safely at a much earlier age. Studies suggest that the practice of early spaying and neutering appears to be safe and does not adversely affect feline maturity, as was once thought. As a result, more and more shelters are opting for early spaying or neutering before they release animals to new homes.

## Spaying

This procedure costs more, because the operation involves opening the abdomen to remove the ovaries, tubes, and uterus. Remember, however, that the one-time cost of spaying a female is still considerably less than the long-term cost of raising and finding homes for successive litters of kittens.

Spaying eliminates the female's annoying heat periods along with her ability to become pregnant. The operation also eliminates the possibility of any disease or infections occurring in the organs removed and decreases the chance that the cat will develop breast cancer later in life.

## Neutering

This is a less invasive procedure that involves removing the testicles. Both surgical procedures require anesthesia, but the postoperative, in-hospital recovery period is generally shorter for males than for females.

Because intact males tend to fight more with other cats, they are more prone than their neutered counterparts to develop abscesses (localized pockets of pus that can be costly to treat) as a result of their frequent, violent encounters. Neutering the male reduces such aggressive behaviors, eliminates testicular

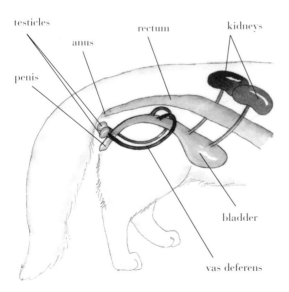

testicles
rectum
kidneys
anus
penis
bladder
vas deferens

*Neutering a male cat makes him unable to reproduce and reduces or eliminates undesirable spraying behaviors.*

*Spaying is a surgical procedure that removes a female cat's ovaries, fallopian tubes, and uterus so that she cannot have kittens.*

diseases, and decreases the chance of disease occurring in other glands affected by male hormones. Neutering also helps curb the pungent odor of tomcat urine, as well as the male cat's bothersome tendency to spray urine in the house to mark his territory.

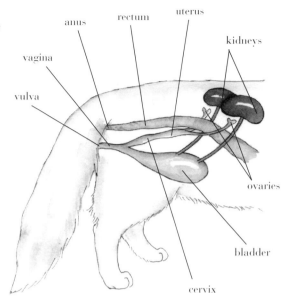

anus
rectum
uterus
kidneys
vagina
vulva
ovaries
bladder
cervix

## Adult or Kitten?

Kittens are cute and adorable, and few people want to miss the joys of this short-lived stage. However, by adopting an adult cat, you may be able to reduce your initial expenses by acquiring one that already has been altered and is up to date on its annual vaccinations.

Certainly, kittenhood holds special joys for cat lovers, but this stage can also be the most destructive. Kittens are not born knowing how you expect them to behave in your home; they have to be properly socialized and patiently taught not to climb your draperies and not to sharpen their claws on your couch.

On the other hand, many adult cats are surrendered to shelters for adoption because of behavior problems related to their past care or to a lack of proper socialization and training. House soiling and destructive clawing are two of the most common behavior problems that result in cats being surrendered to animal shelters for adoption. In many instances, however, owners are forced to give up their adult cats because they must move and can't take the cat with them, or because a family member has developed an allergy to cats.

If you consider an adult cat, do your homework and ask why the animal was put up for adoption. Was it rescued for mistreatment or neglect, or simply abandoned? Did it appear to be lost from its original owner and not reclaimed? Many shelters try to have a history on cats surrendered to them by their owners, but if the animal came in as a stray, its background will remain a mystery. In any case, arrange to take an adult cat on a two-week trial basis, if possible, with the stipulation that you can return it if it doesn't appear to be adjusting well to your home.

## Indoor or Outdoor?

Among the general population, opinions are divided on the issue of indoor versus outdoor cats. Some people insist on letting their cats roam free because they believe that depriving

cats of their outdoor freedom is cruel. Others believe that it is inhumane and irresponsible to willfully subject companion animals to the outdoor hazards of modern urban life.

Regardless of which side of the fence you sit on, the experts agree that cats kept indoors live longer, healthier lives. So, if you want to give your new kitten the best chance of living out its full life span, consider making it a strictly indoor pet. Cats that live their lives totally indoors are less likely to be exposed to diseases, plagued by parasites, hit by cars, attacked by dogs, bitten by wild animals, caught in wild animal traps, poisoned by pesticides, and harmed by cruel people.

You can also expect to have fewer veterinary bills related to injuries from cat fights and similar mishaps if you keep your cat indoors. And you will have peace of mind knowing that your well-cared-for indoor cat has a lesser chance of contracting illness or parasites, such as Lyme

*Red tabby kittens: If you can afford more than one pet, acquire your cats in pairs so they can keep each other company.*

disease-carrying ticks that could affect you or your family.

As long as you provide love and attention, your cat will be quite happy and well adjusted living indoors. If you feel your cat must experience the outdoors, supervise outings in the yard, build an outdoor exercise run, or install a cat flap that provides safe access to a screened-in porch.

If you must have an outdoor cat, or one that spends part of the time indoors and part of the time outside, then adopt one that is already accustomed to this living arrangement. Do *not* adopt an adult cat that has lived all its life indoors and expect it to adjust well to outdoor

survival. On the other hand, outdoor cats can, in many cases, be converted to indoor cats with few problems.

## Longhaired or Shorthaired?

To settle this question, decide how much time you want to spend grooming and vacuuming. Longhaired cats are beautiful, but they require daily grooming to minimize shedding and keep their coats free of mats. As an owner of a longhaired cat, you will also become intimately acquainted with your vacuum cleaner as you try to keep your carpets and furnishings free of loose cat hair. Shorthaired cats shed, too, but not as noticeably. Nor do they require a daily combing and brushing commitment; a few minutes once a week will suffice to rid the coat of loose hairs and keep it clean and shiny.

*Longhaired cats need to be groomed daily to keep their plush coats from matting.*

## Lifestyle Considerations

### Care and Commitment

By now, you realize that acquiring a cat should never be an impulse decision; there are many things you need to consider beforehand. Also, acquiring a cat deserves a commitment on your part to take care of the animal's needs from kittenhood through old age. As mentioned, with modern veterinary care and good nutrition, more cats are living longer, an average 15 to 20 years, so look ahead into your own future and ask yourself if you will be willing and able to provide your cat with shelter, food, and regular veterinary care for a decade or two.

## Housing

Make sure that your housing situation is suitable for owning a cat. If you rent, your landlord may prohibit pets or require an additional fee plus a pet damage deposit. Remember, as a cat owner you are liable and responsible for any property damage or personal injuries your animal may cause.

## Travel and Time Spent Away

Animals, like children, need special attention and someone to look after them when their owners are not around; therefore, before acquiring a cat, consider how much time you normally spend away from home. If you travel often, do you have a trusted friend or relative who will care for your cat while you're away? If not, can you afford to board your cat or hire a pet sitter while you're away?

## Allergies

Many people are allergic to cats, and unfortunately many cats are surrendered to animal shelters each year because their allergic owners cannot tolerate the severity of their allergy symptoms. So, as you consider getting a cat, think about the people close to you who may become uncomfortable living in or visiting your home because their asthma or allergies become more severe in the presence of felines.

## Your Age and Health

Certainly, most people expect to outlive their pets, but this is not guaranteed. Consider what would happen to your cat if you died suddenly or became incapacitated by an injury or illness. Too often, an animal faces neglect, abuse, or abandonment if the owner has not planned ahead for its care in case of an emergency. This is especially true for pet owners who live alone. Give a trusted person advance instructions— and keys—to enter your property immediately and assume care of your cat if you should die suddenly or become disabled. Talk to a lawyer about providing for your cat's care in your will.

# Finding a Mixed Breed

Once you've decided that you want a non-pedigreed cat, the next step is finding a healthy one that's suitable for your home and lifestyle. You should not have to search far, as there is no shortage of cats in need of good homes. To begin, check your local animal shelters, humane society chapters, animal rescue organizations, or cat clubs. Larger organizations are usually listed in the telephone book or advertise in local newspapers. Most veterinarians' offices have information about such organizations, and many even post a list of pets needing homes on their bulletin boards. Other avenues to pursue include the classified section of your local newspaper, pet shops, or friends and neighbors with unplanned litters. Spring is usually the best time to begin looking for a kitten, as this is the season when new litters start arriving, but shelters typically have cats available for adoption year-round.

## Adopting from a Shelter

An animal shelter is an excellent place to find a non-pedigreed cat, but not all shelters are alike. Some are private or volunteer organizations, while others are funded by tax dollars and operated by city or county governments. Generally speaking, an animal control facility is a public institution that must accept any animal brought in. Some animal control facilities, especially those in poorer areas, operate on low budgets and have limited space and, as a result, may be forced to euthanize more animals than they are able to keep and place in homes. Private shelters and volunteer rescue organizations, on the other hand, are more likely to have a "no-kill" policy that they are able to exercise by refusing to accept more animals once they reach capacity, or by using a network of foster homes where cats are cared for until they can be permanently placed.

Adoption practices vary widely, but most shelters will require you to fill out a questionnaire and sign a form agreeing to have the cat spayed or neutered, unless this already has been done. Often, by asking a few questions, the shelter workers can help you select a cat that has a temperament best suited to your own personality and lifestyle. Some shelters may even want to visit your home to ensure that the cat will be housed and cared for properly. Do not be offended by organizations that attempt to investigate your suitability as a pet owner; they are acting in the best interests of the animals they have sworn to protect.

**Shelter fees:** Most shelters also request a donation or charge an adoption fee—usually no more than $50 or $60—to pay for the food and veterinary care the cat received there. If the organization had the animal spayed or neutered, the fee helps cover that cost as well. Another reason shelters charge a fee is that people naturally tend to place greater value on and take better care of a pet that they pay for, as opposed to one that is free.

**Health care:** High-end shelters, or those with bigger budgets to spend, sometimes screen their animals in advance for various parasites and diseases and administer at least an initial series of vaccinations. Some even

spay or neuter animals prior to adoption. Other organizations offer vouchers that can be redeemed at most veterinarians' offices for a free or discounted medical exam and spaying or neutering. Some shelters also operate information hot lines that you can call if you have general questions about cat care and behavior.

Before adopting from a shelter, find out as much as you can about the history and care that has been provided to the cat. For example:
✔ Under what circumstances did the animal arrive at the shelter?
✔ Has a veterinarian examined the cat?
✔ Has it received any vaccinations?
✔ Has it been checked or treated for internal parasites?
✔ Has it been tested and found to be negative for feline leukemia virus (FeLV) and feline immunodeficiency virus (FIV) (see chart, page 55)?

Knowing these details is especially important if you have other cats at home. Usually, this information is spelled out in the contract or adoption agreement that you sign, but if not, always ask. In addition, make sure you understand the shelter's return policy, in case the animal you adopt turns out to be sick or simply doesn't work out in your home.

## Buying from a Pet Shop

Although pet shops usually deal in purebred animals, some do take in unwanted mixed-breed kittens from local residents and sell them. Others will house mixed-breed cats and kittens for local humane societies to improve their chances of adoption. Less scrupulous shops may contract with "backyard" breeders to produce animals for sale. The latter situation is the one you want to avoid, as deliberate

ANIMAL SHELTER
— Adoptions —

*When adopting a cat from an animal shelter, find out as much as you can about the cat's history and previous health care.*

backyard breeding of non-pedigreed animals just compounds the pet overpopulation problem. Buying animals bred for this purpose only encourages more indiscriminate breeding.

If you decide to acquire a cat from a pet shop, select a shop that houses its animals in large cages comfortably furnished with beds, litter pans, toys, and food and water dishes. The accommodations should be clean and odor-free and closed off in such a way—preferably behind glass windows—that customers can look but cannot constantly disturb and handle the kittens.

The staff should be able to tell you the age and sex of the kitten and give you correct advice on cat care. Before buying, try to find out as much as you can about the cat's history. How did the pet shop acquire the cat, for example? If you are satisfied that the staff seems knowledgeable, that the environment is clean, and that the kitten appears healthy, then the pet shop may be as good a place as any to acquire a mixed-breed cat. Just make sure the purchase agreement includes a medical and vaccination history, as well as a suitable return policy.

## Choosing a Healthy Cat

Whether you buy from a pet shop, adopt from a shelter, answer a classified newspaper advertisement, or select a kitten from a neigh-

*If you decide to adopt a stray cat, have it examined by a veterinarian as soon as possible, before risking exposure to other cats that you may have.*

bor's litter, the animal you choose should have good muscle tone and bright, clear eyes, and it should be alert and friendly with a curious or playful attitude. A healthy cat or kitten should not be sneezing or showing mucus discharge around the eyes or nose. The ears should be clean and free of dark, crusty wax. Head shaking or ear scratching may indicate ear mites or other infections. The anus should be clean and free of any signs of diarrhea.

The environment where the cat or kitten has been kept should be clean and free of pungent animal odors. The animal's coat also should be clean and free of fleas. To inspect the coat for fleas, rub your hand against the fur and look for fine grains of black dirt, which is really dried flea excrement, called "flea dirt." Flea signs are more prevalent behind the ears, on

*If you find and adopt a very young, abandoned kitten, your veterinarian may recommend that you bottle-feed it a commercial milk replacer until it is able to eat solid food.*

the back, and at the tail base, where the cat cannot easily reach to lick clean (see page 61 for a discussion of flea allergy dermatitis).

To test the cat's personality, tempt it with a feather or ribbon and see how playful and relaxed it is around strangers. If it appears fearful, hisses at you, cringes from your hand, or, in general, seems unused to being handled, you may want to look elsewhere for a better socialized animal. Of course, a shy, withdrawn cat that huddles quietly at the back of the cage at the animal shelter may come out of its shell and adapt successfully to life with a single adult or a quiet couple. If you have a house full of children, however, you will want to look for an outgoing, unflappable cat, one that sits at the front of the cage and reaches out its paw for attention.

## Medical History

Once you've selected a cat or kitten, ask if it has been tested for FeLV and FIV, as noted previously. If the cat has not been tested, you will want to make sure it is free of these diseases before introducing it to other cats you may have at home. If any medical or vaccination records are available, ask for copies. Have your veterinarian examine the animal within a day or two after you take it home to help ensure that you've picked a healthy one.

## Age

Knowing a kitten's age is important, too. Kittens taken away from their original surroundings too young sometimes suffer from stress and have trouble adjusting to a new environment. Some also may develop unusual behavioral problems related to their maladjustment. Ideally, a kitten should not leave its original environment until it is between 8 and 16 weeks old. By this time, a kitten has been weaned and litter-trained, is eating solid food, and, depending on the owner, may have had some or all of its first year's vaccination series. This is a best-case scenario that may be possible if, for example, you are planning to adopt a kitten from a friend or neighbor's unplanned litter. However, since space at animal shelters is scarce, kittens there typically go to new homes by about eight weeks of age, or as soon as they are weaned and eating solid food.

# Taking in a Stray

Sometimes, it is the cat that finds and "adopts" a new owner, instead of the other way around. We've all heard variations of the typical scenario: A scraggly stray shows up on your doorstep, hungry, perhaps even hurt or sickly. The pathetic plight of such a homeless creature pulls at your heartstrings, so you set food out for it, which is, of course, an invitation to the cat to stay.

Countless cats are cruelly abandoned each year when their owners move, die, or simply grow tired of them and give them the boot. While it's hard to imagine how people can be so irresponsible and cold-hearted as to drop a cat or to move away and abandon the animal to fend for itself, the sad reality is that this happens all too often. Most homeless strays suffer a meager existence and eventually die from disease or starvation, or they end up being hit by cars or killed by other animals. Only a lucky few happen upon the yards and homes of kindhearted folks who eventually take them in.

Before taking in a stray, however, make sure it is genuinely homeless, and not just a neighborhood pet looking for an extra handout. Ask around or advertise in the Lost and Found section of your newspaper. If the cat is lost, the original owner may come forward and claim it. If the cat is tame enough to let you handle it without it scratching and biting you, check for any form of pet identification—collar, ear tag, or tattoo (usually on a rear inner thigh). Some owners have tiny microchips implanted between the pet's shoulder blades. These can be detected by a special scanner, which your area's animal shelter may have.

## Precautions to Take

If you do happen to acquire a homeless stray, there are some special precautions you should take:

**1.** Assume that the cat has had no vaccinations, including rabies, and approach the animal cautiously, for your safety.

**2.** Wear thick gloves when you try to pick up the animal the first time. Many abandoned cats revert to the wild after only a short period without human contact, and they will fight fiercely if captured.

**3.** If you have other cats, do not expose them to the stray until it has been checked by a veterinarian and quarantined from your animals for at least a week.

**4.** Before bringing the stray into your home, capture it, place it in a carrier, and take it to a veterinarian immediately for a thorough examination.

If you intend to keep the animal, request that it be checked for parasites and tested for FeLV and FIV. If the latter tests come back positive, you will be faced with a difficult decision, as you will not want to take an infected animal home and expose it to your other healthy cats. If you have no other cats at home, you will want to weigh the costs of providing ongoing medical care for a sick animal before you definitely decide to keep it. FeLV- and FIV-infected cats can live a long time with their chronic conditions. Your veterinarian can tell you what to expect.

If the animal checks out as healthy, have it vaccinated for rabies and feline respiratory diseases right away, and follow any other vaccination plan your veterinarian recommends. If the cat is an intact male, have him neutered to reduce the incidence of spraying and fighting. In the case of a female foundling, it may be difficult to tell whether she has already been spayed, so you may want to keep her inside and wait awhile to see whether she goes into heat or displays any signs of pregnancy.

## Rehabilitating a Sickly Stray

If the cat is ill or malnourished, your veterinarian can recommend an appropriate treatment plan. If the stray appears to have a potentially contagious respiratory illness, you may want to consider boarding it at the clinic until it recovers, rather than risk exposing your other cats at home. This will also allow time for all of the necessary test results to come back.

If you've found an abandoned kitten, chances are it may be dehydrated and will require fluid replacement. If the kitten was orphaned at a young age and is weak from malnutrition and neglect, you may be in for a siege of round-the-clock feedings every few hours. Newborns must be fed every two or three hours, and because they cannot yet eliminate on their own, you will need to stimulate the anal area with a warm, moist washcloth after feeding. Normally, the mother cat performs this duty by licking her youngsters' bottoms with her rough, wet tongue. By about four weeks of age, kittens can control their own elimination. At that time, they also can begin experimenting with soft, solid foods. Whatever the circumstances, your veterinarian can recommend an appropriate formula and feeding schedule.

The outcome of such rescues is always unpredictable and sometimes downright sad, but the rewards can be potentially great, as the survivors often seem to comprehend their predicament. Eternally grateful to their human benefactors, these rescued cats often turn out to be the most devoted and loving companions of all.

# BRINGING YOUR MIXED BREED HOME

## Basic Cat Supplies

Bringing home a new cat or kitten is an exciting time for the whole family, but the sudden change to new surroundings may be somewhat intimidating from the new arrival's viewpoint. To make your cat's transition to its new home as comfortable as possible, a little planning and preparation are in order. You'll need to have on hand:

✔ some cat or kitten food (see page 37)
✔ a cat carrier
✔ food and water dishes
✔ a litter box and filler
✔ a litter scoop
✔ a scratching post
✔ a cat bed
✔ some cat toys

## Pet Carrier

To bring your kitten home, you'll need a suitable cat carrier for the animal to travel safely in. This item is essential for carting your cat to the veterinarian or boarding facility. Available at pet supply stores, and sometimes at veterinarians' offices, pet carriers range from inexpensive fold-out cardboard boxes to the sturdier molded plastic ones. There are also

*Children need to be taught how to hold and handle cats gently.*

wicker baskets and canvas totebag varieties. If you ever need to take your cat on an airplane, the airlines will specify the dimensions and type of pet carrier required in the cabin or in the cargo hold. Regardless of the carrier type you select, it should fasten securely and be well ventilated so that the animal inside cannot escape but can get plenty of fresh air.

If you have more than one cat, each animal should have its own carrier for safe transport. Avoid putting two cats together in a single carrier, even if they are best friends. The too-tight quarters and the stress of travel might cause them to fight and injure one another.

## Food and Water Dishes

Every pet in the household should have its own feeding dish, so select one ahead of time for your new cat and decide on a feeding location. Stainless steel, ceramic stoneware, or glass dishes, although more expensive than plastic feeding bowls, are generally easier to keep clean because they can be sterilized in the dishwasher without melting or warping. Ceramic dishes come in decorative varieties, but select only the ones sold for human use or labeled as lead-free.

Although they are less expensive, plastic dishes tend to develop tiny pits and scratches over time, which can harbor bacteria and odors, despite diligent cleaning. The stale food odors that collect in these minute crevices may go unnoticed by the human nose, but your cat, with its more highly developed sense of smell, may find the odor buildup offensive enough to refuse to eat. To deter odor buildup, buy plastic dishes that are dishwasher-safe so they can be heat-sterilized between meals. Another sound precaution is to periodically replace plastic dishes with new ones.

When selecting feeding dishes, keep in mind that most cats seem to prefer flat, shallow saucers or plates to deep bowls. Some cats dislike having their sensitive whiskers rub the sides of the dish as they eat, and to avoid the unpleasant sensation, they will resort to scooping out food morsels with their paws and eating off the floor.

Also, choose a weighted food dish that's heavy enough to stay put and not slide across the floor as the cat eats. Imagine how frustrating your meals would be if your plate kept sliding across the table every time you tried to take a bite!

## Litter Box

This is essential equipment for any cat that spends time indoors. Pet stores and mail-order catalogs carry a wide variety of litter pans, from the basic open plastic models to the fancy ones with ventilated bottoms and pull-out trays.

For privacy, place the litter box in a quiet, undisturbed area of the house. Do not place it too near the cat's food dishes or sleeping quarters. Being fastidious creatures, cats normally do not like to eat or sleep near the place where they relieve themselves.

If you have more than one cat, provide each with its own litter box, and place the pans in separate locations, if necessary. Although cat friends will often share litter pans, some more

aggressive cats may chase others away in a show of dominance. Without an alternate box to use, the subordinate cat may have no choice but to use the carpet or some other inappropriate place.

By the time your kitten is old enough to leave its mother and go to its new home, it should already know how to use a litter box. The instinctive digging and covering behaviors come naturally to cats, and they learn the rest by observing and imitating their mothers.

Generally, all you have to do is show the kitten where its new litter box is. Do this when you first bring the kitten home and again after the kitten's first few meals in its new surroundings, and it should quickly catch onto the idea. If the kitten seems slow to catch on, it may be necessary to confine it temporarily to a small area with a litter box, until it does its business. Sometimes adding a single drop of ammonia to the litter helps. The scent of ammonia, being a by-product of urine, usually attracts cats to use the spot as a potty.

## Cat Litter

The type of cat box filler you select for the litter pan is important, because if your cat doesn't like the texture or scent of the type you choose, it may refuse to use the box. Some cats dislike the perfumed or chemically treated pellets that are added to commercial litters for odor control. These additives may please human noses, but cats seem to prefer their own scent. For really finicky felines, plain, untreated clay litter or sterilized sand may be better choices. Avoid using dirt from the yard or garden, however, as it may contain insect larvae or other unwanted organisms, including the one that causes *toxoplasmosis* (see page 35).

Some litter brands are designed to clump when moistened, making it easier to scoop out clumps of urine along with the solid wastes. This clumping action aids greatly in sanitation and odor control by leaving behind only clean, fresh litter.

Certain clumping brands have an unfortunate tendency to stick to a cat's fur, although many manufacturers have worked to correct this problem. If you have a longhaired cat, inspect the backside and hind legs on occasion to make sure litter is not sticking to your cat's fur.

In addition, concerns have been raised about clumping litters causing digestive blockages, if swallowed. As a precaution, avoid using a clumping litter with young kittens, as they are more likely than adults to sample the stuff by tasting and eating it; then, when your cat is grown, switch to a convenient clumping brand if you like.

Most litter brands cannot be flushed down toilets, so, to avoid ruining your bathroom plumbing, read product labels carefully.

## Litter Scoop

Keep the litter box clean; if the box becomes too dirty or offensive, the cat may stop using it and start soiling the house. The most effective and least expensive way to control litter box odor in your home is to scoop wastes from the box daily and change the litter frequently. A little bit of baking soda sprinkled on and stirred into the litter also helps control odor in close quarters. Or try one of several commercial cat box odor control products available at pet supply and grocery stores.

## Scratching Post

A sturdy scratching post is another essential piece of equipment for any cat confined to the indoors. Cats have an instinctive need to scratch and sharpen their claws on objects in their territory. Even declawed cats continue to display this natural feline behavior. The action not only removes dead nails and reconditions the claws but also marks territory with scent from glands in the paw pads. You cannot eliminate the cat's natural instinct to sharpen claws, but you can contain the behavior by providing your cat with a scratching post.

Pet shops and pet supply catalogs sell scratching posts in many shapes and sizes. Carpeted cat trees that extend from floor to ceiling make attractive scratching posts and come in all colors to match any room's decor. Creative designs incorporate built-in perches and peekaboo penthouses for catnapping. Not only do they double as lofty sleeping quarters, they offer ample exercise and climbing opportunities for indoor cats.

Before introducing your cat to its scratching post, make sure the post isn't wobbly and won't tip over as the cat claws it. Obviously, if a flimsy, unstable post falls over and frightens your cat, the animal likely will refuse to go near it ever again—understandably so. The base must be wide and supportive enough to remain standing and balanced, even when accosted by the full weight of a clawing, jumping, or climbing adult cat.

Introduce your cat to the scratching post at an early age, or as soon as you bring the newcomer into your home. Simply show the cat the post, move its paws in a scratching motion, and praise lavishly when it does what you want. If necessary, rub some dried catnip on the post to entice your cat to play and climb on it. If the cat decides to try out your furniture, scold verbally by saying *"No"* in a loud,

*A sturdy pet carrier is a must for safe transport to the veterinarian's office or elsewhere.*

sharp tone. Or squirt jets of clean water from a water pistol to startle the cat without harming it. Wait a few minutes, then carry the cat to its scratching post.

Once clawing the furniture becomes an established habit, it is difficult to break, but not impossible. The recommended strategy is to make the inappropriate surface unattractive to the cat while, at the same time, offering a

more appealing, acceptable substitute, such as a suitable scratching post. To discourage an undesirable scratching habit, cover the problem area temporarily with a loosely draped blanket, newspaper, wrapping paper, plastic bubble wrap, or sheets of aluminum foil. Then, as previously explained, consistently encourage the cat to use the acceptable substitute.

Cats are easy to train and readily learn to respond to voice tones and commands. If you are consistent and persistent in your methods, your cat should soon learn to restrict its clawing to the designated area. When disciplining your cat, use your voice, but never, *never* strike the animal with your hand, with a folded newspaper, or with any other object. Such abusive action will only make your cat fearful and distrustful of humans.

## Cat Bed

Most cats like to select their own sleeping places and will alternate their napping spots on a whim. More than likely, your cat's preferred siesta site will be *your* bed or your favorite chair. Many people like to share their beds with their cats. However, if you want to discourage your cat from sleeping with you, keep your

*Kittens learn to use the litter box by watching their mother. Sometimes kittens that are abandoned or taken away from their mother too young develop sloppy toilet habits because they missed the opportunity to learn proper cat behaviors from Mom.*

*Many cats like to sleep on their owner's bed or a favorite chair, but this brown tabby looks quite comfortable in his own padded wicker basket.*

bedroom door shut or confine your cat to a certain area of the house during the night.

Regardless of your preferred sleeping arrangements, provide your cat with its own bed for daytime as well as nighttime napping. Whether you buy a plush, fancy cat "cozy" from the pet store or simply throw an old blanket in a cardboard box, select something washable, because you want to be able to launder your cat's bedding frequently.

## Safe Cat Toys

Indoor cats need toys to play with, but you don't have to spend a lot of money on them. Cats can amuse themselves with ordinary items you might use in your own recreational pursuits, such as Ping-Pong balls, golf balls, and tennis balls. Leftover wrapping paper and paper gro-

cery bags are a great favorite, too, but *never* use plastic bags for this purpose or leave them unattended around your cat, because cats, like children, may suffocate in them. A cardboard box with cut-out peep holes is another inexpensive toy that can give your cat hours of delight.

When selecting toys at the pet store, consider safety first:

**1.** Choose only sturdy toys that won't disintegrate after the first few mock attacks.

**2.** Remove tied-on bells, plastic eyes, button noses, and dangling strings that your cat could tear off and swallow or choke on during play.

**Warning:** Never let your cat play with small items that could be chewed or swallowed easily, such as buttons, bows, hairpins, rubber bands, wire bread-wrapper ties, paper clips, cellophane, or wadded-up candy wrappers.

**3.** Supervise all access to fishing pole-style toys with feathers, sparklers, and tied-on lures. These interactive toys provide great exercise in your watchful presence, but if left unattended, the attached line poses a potential hazard for being chewed or swallowed, for accidental strangulation, or for getting wrapped too tightly around a limb and cutting off vital circulation. Always shut these types of toys safely away in a closet when you're not around to play with and supervise your cat.

4. String of any kind is a definite no-no for cats; do not offer yarn balls or threaded spools as toys. If you use such items in crafts or hobbies, store them safely out of reach of your cat.

5. Also, be careful of braided rugs or knitted afghans that might unravel if the cat plays with a loose end. Once a cat starts chewing and swallowing string or yarn, a considerable amount may amass in the digestive tract and cause life-threatening blockages or perforations. If you come home to find your cat with a piece of string hanging out of its mouth, *do not* attempt to pull it out. Doing so can cause more serious, even fatal, injury if the string has already wound its way into the intestinal tract. *Seek veterinary help immediately!* Such a situation constitutes a true emergency. Surgery may be required to correct the ensuing condition, called *string enteritis*.

## Catnip, the Natural High

A member of the mint family, catnip is a perennial herb that many cats go wild over. When exposed to a catnip-scented toy, a cat will grip the object in its front paws, rub its face in the fabric, and roll ecstatically, kicking at the object with the back paws. Afterward, the cat lies sprawled on its back, as if drunk, and dozes off in a relaxed, trancelike state of bliss, purring loudly and contentedly.

The substance in the plant that elicits this response is called nepetalactone. The effect wears off in a short time and does not appear to compromise the cat's normal faculties; in fact, an unfamiliar sound will bring a catnip-intoxicated cat to its fully alert senses immediately. Pet stores offer an array of catnip mice, catnip sacks, and other catnip-scented toys for your cat's pleasure. Some stores even sell planter kits so you can grow your own stand of catnip at home.

The catnip herb is not thought to be addictive or harmful to domestic cats, so it is a relatively safe way to entice even the most sedate feline into a feisty, albeit brief, bout of play; however, not all cats care for catnip, and many have only a mild response when exposed to it. Some cats lack the gene that makes them respond to the plant's intoxicating effects, and they show no marked reaction when confronted with catnip.

# A Cat-safe Home

## Indoor Hazards

Because cats are such clean creatures, they can ingest wax, bleach, detergents, and other toxic chemicals stored inside your home; all an unsuspecting cat need do is simply brush against a dirty storage container, or walk through a spill, then lick the offending substance off its paws and fur as it self-grooms. With this in mind, take an inventory of all household chemicals and other potential hazards in your home that a climbing, exploring cat might have access to.

While it's hard to think of everything, be creative when you are scanning your home for potential hazards. To make your home cat-safe, do the same things you would do to make it child-safe.

Here are some suggestions for cat-proofing your home:

✔ **Electric cords:** Chewing on electrical cords can result in burns and electric shock. To prevent this, tuck electrical and telephone cords out of reach under mats or carpets, tack or tape them down, or cover them with PVC piping. Coating cords with bitter apple, bitter lime (available at pet stores), raw onion juice, or Tabasco sauce also helps discourage chewing.

✔ **Drapery cords:** Keep window and drapery cords tied up and well out of reach, as a frolicking feline can become entangled in dangling cords and accidentally hang or strangle itself.

✔ **Flimsy screening:** Make sure all window and door screens are strong, sturdy, and secure enough to prevent a cat from pushing them out or falling through them.

✔ **Fireplaces:** Securely screen fireplaces so that, when in use, cats cannot get near the flames.

✔ **Household chemicals:** Store cleaners, laundry detergents, fabric softeners, solvents, mothballs, insect sprays, and all other household chemicals out of reach in securely closed cabinets.

✔ **Cosmetics and medicines:** Keep perfumes, cosmetics, nail polish removers, and all vitamins and medicines, including aspirin and acetaminophen (highly toxic to cats), tightly capped and put away.

✔ **String and hobby supplies:** Put away pins, needles, yarns, spools of thread, artists' paints, and other hobby and crafts supplies when not in use to prevent a curious cat from investigating them and accidentally swallowing something harmful.

✔ **Hazardous toys:** Certain children's toys can pose potential dangers to your cat. For example, an indoor basketball hoop placed over a trash can may trap a curious kitten that climbs or falls into the netting, causing accidental strangulation.

✔ **Vermin bait:** Avoid placing edible rodent and insect baits where your cat might get at them and be poisoned.

✔ **Breakables:** Remove or secure all glass or breakable items on tables, shelves, and bookcases that an exploring cat might knock over.

✔ **Toilets and sump pumps:** Keep toilet lids down and cover sump pumps so that kittens can't fall in and drown.

✔ **Appliances:** Before shutting the door of any major appliance, such as the dryer or refrigerator, look to make sure your cat hasn't jumped in unnoticed. Unplug small appliances when not in use and tuck cords out of the way. A cat playing with a dangling cord can topple a lamp or pull a small appliance off a counter onto itself.

✔ **Stoves and countertops:** Supervise all kitchen activities. With a cat in the house, no countertop is safe from exploring paws. If an inquisitive cat should leap up on the stove top when you're not looking, it can get burned accidentally by stepping on a hot burner or by sniffing a boiling saucepan or tea kettle.

✔ **Trash cans:** Keep tight-fitting lids on all (indoor and outdoor) trash bins so that foraging cats won't get sick from spoiled foodstuffs or injured by discarded razor blades, broken glass, or jagged tin can edges.

✔ **Houseplants:** Although carnivorous by nature, cats enjoy snacking on greenery, apparently because the added roughage aids in digestion. Unfortunately, cats often indulge this occasional craving by nibbling on decorative houseplants and ornamental shrubs. While many plants are harmless to cats, others are deadly. Ingestion can cause a wide range of symptoms, including mouth irritation, drooling,

*Cats often are depicted playing with balls of yarn; however, allowing cats to play with string of any kind is an unsafe practice that can lead to "string enteritis," a potentially fatal intestinal blockage caused by swallowed string.*

tinsel, angel hair, and artificial snow. Ingesting these items can be potentially dangerous for cats, so either avoid using them or restrict your cat's access to the decorated rooms.

vomiting, diarrhea, hallucinations, convulsions, lethargy, and coma. If your cat displays any unusual behavior after chewing on a plant, consult a veterinarian immediately. The National Animal Poison Control Information Center also offers a comprehensive list of plants toxic to cats. The center's number is listed in the back of this book (page 92).

✔ **Holiday decorations:** Although accidental poisonings can happen any time of the year, they seem to be more prevalent during the year-end holidays. That's because cats like to investigate and sometimes sample the greenery and decorations commonly used for holiday decorations—poinsettia, holly berries, mistletoe,

## Outdoor Hazards

Even though you may have wisely decided to keep your cat safely indoors, there likely will be times when you will want to allow it outside for short periods with supervision. When you do so, be aware that there are many potential hazards as close as your backyard and driveway. Here are some to remember:

✔ **Lawn care products:** Pesticides, weed killers, fungicides, and fertilizers can poison pets that walk in treated areas, then lick the chemicals off their paws, so read lawn care and pesticide product labels carefully before using. Avoid letting your cat outdoors to pad through freshly treated areas until the first rain or the next thorough watering has rinsed away the substance.

✔ **Pools and ponds:** Supervise pets around swimming pools and ponds, just as you would a child. Although cats can swim, kittens, especially, can drown from exhaustion if they fall in and can't find a way to climb out of the water.

✔ **Antifreeze leaks:** The driveway is another area where special precautions should be

*Many indoor and outdoor plants are toxic to cats. Ask your veterinarian for a list.*

*Window screens in your home must be strong and sturdy in case your indoor cat decides to climb after a flittering bug on the outside.*

observed. Ethylene glycol, the prime ingredient in traditional antifreeze, is deadly poisonous to animals. As little as half a teaspoon can kill an adult cat, so if your car has even a tiny cooling system leak, you may put your own cat, or your neighbors' pets, at risk. To avoid this, immediately hose down or wipe up all fluid leaks and antifreeze spills, no matter how small. When adding fluids to your car, use a funnel to prevent spills.

Consider replacing your car's traditional antifreeze with a safer antifreeze brand. Safer antifreeze products on the market contain *propylene glycol,* which is significantly less toxic than ethylene glycol. In fact, propylene glycol is used as a preservative in some foods, alcoholic beverages, cosmetics, and pharmaceuticals. Even though your cat is an indoor cat, using a safer antifreeze is a humane practice that can benefit free-roaming domestic animals and wildlife.

## Your Cat and Other Pets

Being sociable and adaptable animals, cats generally learn to get along well with other pets. Before exposing a new animal to other cats you already own, have the newcomer checked by a veterinarian and tested for parasites and contagious diseases, especially feline leukemia virus (FeLV) and feline immune deficiency virus (FIV) (see chart, page 55).

*To prevent your cat from going fishing, cover aquariums with a hood and keep gold fish bowls out of reach.*

While awaiting the test results, keep the new arrival isolated from your other pets, in a separate room or in a cage. This also allows time for the "house smell" to settle on the newcomer, which may help make the introductions less

threatening. After a few days, remove the new cat from its separate quarters for a while and let the resident pets go in and sniff the new scent. When the time seems right, allow the resident pets to see and sniff the newcomer, but supervise all contact for the first few weeks. Keep dogs on a leash during these first meetings so they won't chase and frighten the newcomer. Gradually increase the exposure time until the pets seem to settle down and become acquainted.

Although it's usually easier to introduce a kitten, rather than a grown cat, into a home that already has a feline, don't be dismayed if it takes as long as a month for the animals to accept each other and become friends. Cats are territorial creatures, and adding a newcomer to the environment means that new boundaries must be set. In time, the tension usually disappears. However, cats, like people, are individuals, and occasionally two turn out to be simply incompatible.

If you have rabbits, guinea pigs, birds, or other small pets, it's possible to achieve harmony among different species as long as you provide secure, separate living quarters for all and supervise any direct contact. While there have been reports of cats and pet birds striking up unusual friendships, it is never wise to leave an adult cat alone with uncaged birds or small animals of prey. Cats are natural predators, and it is neither fair nor reasonable to expect them to ignore or control their instincts under such circumstances.

# Cats and Children

Children find kittens irresistible, but they have to be taught how to handle them properly. Not only can a child injure a fragile kitten, but an animal that is frightened or annoyed by a child's unintentional roughness may defend itself by scratching or biting the child. To avoid such mishaps, teach your child that pets are not animated toys, and supervise all physical contact between small children and pets. If the child pulls on a cat's tail or ears, remove the child's hand and show him or her how to gently stroke the animal's fur. Explain to your child that loud screams and sudden movements may frighten the cat. Show your child where cats like to be stroked most—under the chin, behind the ears, and on the neck and back. Explain that some cats do not like to be stroked on their stomachs and rumps, while others will tolerate it from people they know well and trust. Teach your child how to properly pick up and hold a cat.

## Picking Up a Cat

The proper way to pick up a cat is to put one hand under the chest behind the forelegs and the other hand under the rump to support the rear legs and body. Cradle the cat in your arms against your chest. Your cat will let you know when it wants down. Some cats do not like being held and will struggle in your arms to get down.

Although mother cats carry their kittens by the scruff of the neck, this method is not recommended. Carrying by the neck scruff can injure an adult cat if not done properly and should be reserved for emergency restraint. Even then, care must be taken to fully support the cat's rear legs and body weight with the other hand. Allowing the cat's full weight to dangle without such support can seriously injure those neck and back muscles—and *never* lift a cat by its ears or its front paws.

*To pick up and hold a cat properly, place one hand behind the front legs and support the rear legs with your other hand. Then cradle the cat upright in your arms against your chest.*

## Cats and Babies

Couples planning a family often ask whether they can keep their cat and still have a baby. We've all heard those ridiculous "old wives' tales" about cats sucking milk from infants' mouths and smothering them. Certainly, it's wise not to allow your cat to have unsupervised access to an infant, not because there's any truth to those silly old wives' tales, but because a baby's screams, cries, or jerky movements may frighten the cat and result in accidental scratching or biting. If necessary, install a screen door at the nursery entrance. Also, to keep cats out of the cradle, consider buying a mesh crib tent. Baby supply stores sell these as well as cat nets that cover playpens and strollers.

*Toxoplasmosis* deserves a mention here, because it's one of those scary reasons well-meaning people bring up to convince mothers-to-be that their cats must go before a new baby comes. If you're planning to have a baby, get the facts first from your obstetrician and veterinarian. Tests are available to detect the disease, which is caused by a protozoan. Studies indicate that most people already have a degree of immunity to the disease, but if a pregnant woman is exposed to it for the first time, birth defects can occur.

Of course, a cat has to acquire the disease first before it can pass it on to a human being. Cats get the disease by eating infected birds, rodents, or raw meat, then they shed the eggs in their feces. Humans can get the disease by handling soil or litter contaminated by the feces of an infected cat. The majority of cases in humans, however, are not the result of contact with cats, but instead can be traced to people eating undercooked meat.

Cats can be tested for the disease, and if found to be free of the infection there's no cause for worry. If your cat never roams outdoors, never hunts, eats prepackaged commercial pet foods, and is never fed raw or undercooked meat, the chances of it ever acquiring the disease are virtually nonexistent.

If you become pregnant or plan to, discuss this important issue with your doctor. When you know the facts and observe sensible precautions—such as thoroughly cooking all meats before eating, washing your hands after handling raw meats, and wearing gloves when gardening or cleaning the cat box—there's generally no need whatsoever to give up your cat if you're going to have a baby.

# FEEDING YOUR MIXED BREED

## Life-cycle Nutrition

Good nutrition is a relative term that depends a great deal on a cat's age, activity level, and current state of health. What's good for a kitten is not necessarily the best choice for an older cat, and vice versa. Research has shown that certain nutrients consumed at too high or too low levels during early life stages may contribute to health problems in later life. This knowledge ended the old womb-to-tomb practice of feeding cats one food their entire lives, and ushered in a new era of life-cycle nutrition.

Today's pet food labels state whether the product is formulated for *growth and reproduction, adult maintenance*, or for *all life stages* of the cat. Most manufacturers make product lines geared to all three.

*Growth and reproduction* formulas are made specifically to satisfy the extra nutrient requirements of growing kittens and pregnant or nursing queens (female cats). Foods formulated for *all life stages of cats* meet these same requirements because they must satisfy the range of

*Dry and semimoist cat foods can be left out all day without spoiling. Free-choice feeding allows your cat to nibble small meals at will throughout the day, a recommended feeding method unless your cat tends to overeat.*

nutritional needs for cats of all ages; however, *adult maintenance* formulas are intended primarily for fully grown, nonbreeding, and generally less active felines. This means that foods labeled for adult maintenance do not have to meet the higher nutrient requirements of growth and reproduction formulas. For this reason, adult maintenance diets are *not* satisfactory fare for kittens or pregnant cats.

### Feeding Kittens

For its first full year, your kitten needs a greater amount of high-quality protein for growth than it will require in adulthood. At least 30 to 40 percent of a kitten's diet should be protein. Select a kitten or feline growth formula designed to meet this extra need. Follow the feeding guidelines on the package, adjusting the portions as needed. In general, you should let growing kittens eat as much as they seem to want.

While a high-quality food formulated for *all life stages of cats* is also adequate, dry foods formulated for growth and reproduction are usually molded into smaller morsels that make it easier for smaller mouths to chew. Kittens require more frequent feedings, but in smaller quantities, than adult cats. Newly weaned kittens need three or four feedings a day. By about age six months, two meals a day should suffice.

## Feeding Moderately Active Cats

Adult, nonbreeding cats need enough nutrients, fiber, and protein to satisfy their appetites, yet prevent them from getting fat. While a food formulated for *all life stages of cats* may be fine for many adult felines, some cats tend to become overweight in their middle years as their activity level declines, starting at age six or seven. For moderately active adults, a suitable commercial food formulated for *adult maintenance* may be an appropriate choice, especially if your cat stays indoors and tends to be a little overweight. Your veterinarian can best assess your cat's weight, body condition, and nutritional needs at any given age, and recommend an appropriate diet.

Because adult maintenance formulas contain less protein than the growth and reproduction foods, or foods formulated for all life stages, they are *not* suitable for growing kittens or pregnant cats. They are, however, adequate for a moderately active, nonbreeding adult cat's lower energy requirements.

## Feeding Senior Cats

Foods labeled *for all life stages* are designed to meet the needs of all cats, from kittens to senior citizens. However, older, less active cats often require fewer calories, less salt, and less protein than these diets may contain. Cats with special health concerns, such as kidney or heart disease, may also require one of several therapeutic diets available through veterinarians.

Still other cats in their advanced years, although in relatively good health, may start getting thin because their bodies are no longer able to digest and use nutrients from their food as well as when they were young. To maintain their weight and condition, some of these older cats—as long as they're healthy and not suffering from kidney disease or other medical problems—may thrive better on a highly digestible or energy-dense food to help make up for the nutrients their bodies are wasting. Many premium foods are formulated for greater digestibility, which results in less waste of nutrients. In some cases, a high-quality kitten or growth formula may even be appropriate for an otherwise healthy older cat. Such a choice would *not* be appropriate, however, if your veterinarian determines that old age or disease has compromised your elder cat's kidney function. Instead, the veterinarian may recommend a special, therapeutic diet with only moderate levels of high-quality protein to ease the burden on the kidneys.

Remember, your veterinarian is the best judge of your cat's overall condition and dietary needs. Weight loss and other changes in your cat's condition need to be evaluated medically to rule out underlying causes, such as kidney failure or thyroid disease. Cats are generally considered *seniors* at about age ten, but before your cat reaches the decade mark, ask your veterinarian to reassess the animal's dietary needs and recommend any appropriate changes in feeding rations and routine. As a pet owner, it is your responsibility to ask pertinent questions about your cat's health at each annual checkup and to keep your veterinarian honestly informed about your cat's general care and eating habits.

# Avoid Finicky Behavior

Well known for their finicky eating habits, cats have a discriminating sense of taste. Once developed, their taste preferences and finicky behavior can be difficult to change. A cat fed the same type or flavor of food all its life may steadfastly refuse any sort of dietary change, even if its health depends on it.

To avoid creating finicky eating behavior, and to provide variety and appetite appeal, select two or three high-quality products your cat seems to like and use them interchangeably. For example, many owners find it convenient to feed a serving of canned food in the morning and leave out dry food for free-choice nibbling throughout the day. Alternating a few varieties of cat foods and flavors in this way from kittenhood on will go a long way toward preventing your cat from becoming addicted to one type of food.

# Cat Food Types

Commercial pet foods come in three basic types: canned, semimoist (also called soft-dry), and dry. Each type comes in a variety of flavors as well, and each has some advantages and disadvantages to consider before you settle on a favorite.

### Canned Foods

Canned foods are generally the most palatable to the feline taste buds, and often the most expensive type to buy, from the human consumer's standpoint. Finicky eaters seem to prefer canned foods and will often select them over dry foods. Canned foods taste better because they contain more protein and fat than either dry or semimoist foods, which enhances their palatability.

*For variety, give your cat a daily serving of canned food and leave out dry food for your cat to nibble at will.*

Canned foods also contain more moisture than either dry or semimoist foods, making them a better choice for cats that need more water due to some medical condition, such as kidney disease. For cats that have missing teeth or sore gums due to dental disease, canned foods are also ideal because they require virtually no chewing.

Single-serving cans, although more expensive, result in less waste than using the larger cans, because many cats will refuse to eat canned food after it has been refrigerated. Having evolved as predators, cats prefer their food warm, at the average body temperature of small prey animals or, at least, at normal room temperature. So always warm refrigerated leftovers before serving. When warming leftovers in the microwave oven, test the portion with your finger before serving to make sure it is not too hot. A cat that burns its mouth on hot food will probably refuse that type or variety the next time.

To avoid spoilage and odors, take up any uneaten portions of canned food as soon as the cat finishes eating. Canned foods will spoil quickly and attract insects if left out too long, so free-choice feeding is not an option with this type.

## Semimoist Foods

Semimoist foods attempt to combine some benefits of the dry and canned types, making them an attractive, middle-of-the-road choice for human consumers to use for their cats. These foods typically come in soft-dry nuggets packaged in foil-lined wrappers or bags. They contain more moisture than dry foods, but they lack the odors of canned foods that human consumers so often find offensive. Unlike canned rations, semimoist foods can be left out all day without spoiling, allowing the cat to nibble at will, which is the way most cats prefer to eat.

Unlike dry foods, however, semimoist products are too soft to help reduce dental tartar. The

*For their first full year, kittens need a commercial cat food formulated for growth and reproduction, or a food that meets the nutritional requirements of "all life stages" of the cat.*

convenience packaging is a major advantage, because the single-serving foil pouches take the guesswork out of controlled-portion feeding.

At one time, semimoist cat food products contained a chemical preservative called *propylene glycol*, which is the same substance used in safer (*not* traditional) antifreeze brands (see page 33 for information on antifreeze poisoning). This chemical also appears in many cosmetics, medicines, and alcoholic beverages used by humans; however, its use is no longer allowed in cat food products, because it has been implicated in causing red blood cell damage in cats.

## Dry Foods

Of the three basic types, dry foods are generally the least expensive to buy and the most convenient to serve. They are not as smelly as canned foods, and they can be left out all day without spoiling for cats to eat at will. Called *ad libitum* or free-choice feeding, this method is often recommended in the product-feeding guidelines on dry food package labels.

Unfortunately, many owners make the mistake of leaving out too much dry food, encouraging their cats to overeat and grow fat. Instead of putting out bulk amounts of dry food that could last for several days, it is best to carefully measure out each meal or each day's portion, using the product feeding recommendations as a guide. By leaving out controlled portions of dry food for free-choice nibbling, you are less likely to end up with a fat cat (see page 46 for more information on obesity in cats).

At one time, it was thought that letting cats nibble on dry foods throughout the day predisposed them to a potentially life-threatening lower urinary tract condition called *feline urologic syndrome* (FUS) (see page 50) by allowing the urine pH to become too alkaline. Now, with improved pet food products on the market,

*Offering a variety of commercial food types and textures can help prevent your cat from getting "addicted" to one specific brand and becoming a finicky eater.*

reformulated with acidifying ingredients to better maintain urine pH levels within normal acidic ranges, free-choice feeding is no longer the hotly debated issue it once was in this regard.

Dry foods also may benefit cats by promoting better dental health. Although this issue, too, has been widely debated, it is generally believed that the hard chewing action required with dry foods helps scour the teeth and gums, and thus aids in controlling ugly tartar buildup that can lead to gum disease and tooth loss. Some new dry food varieties are specifically formulated to promote more chewing action, and thus greater dental benefits. However, because cats tend to swallow their food almost whole, the benefits

of such chewing action should never be considered a substitute for routine dental care performed by your veterinarian.

# Cat Food Brands

Aside from the basic food types, cat foods are also packaged and marketed according to whether they are generic (economy brands), popular, or premium brands.

## Economy Brands

While the less expensive generic foods, which are typically sold under a private label or store name, tend to be lower in quality and use poorer-grade ingredients, this is not always true. Sometimes it is cheaper for a manufacturer to simply stick a generic label on a popular brand and market it under a different name without changing the formula. Before choosing a generic brand, however, you should contact the manufacturer and thoroughly research the product ingredients.

## Supermarket Brands

The nationally advertised, popular name-brand products are sold in supermarkets, while the more expensive premium brands are sold primarily through pet supply stores and veterinarians' offices. Other than price, some popular and premium brands may differ very little. There is no industry-regulated definition for what a *premium* or a *super-premium* product should be and no higher nutritional standard that premium pet foods must adhere to. These words are simply descriptive marketing tools.

The general assumption is, however, that premium foods contain higher-quality ingredients and remain stable in their makeup, whereas popular brands are more likely to change recipe ingredients according to the current market cost and availability of those ingredients.

## Premium Brands

Premium products also are often marketed as being more digestible and *energy dense,* which means that a smaller amount is required per serving to provide the necessary nutrients. Another general assumption is that the product research behind premium brands is more substantial. While this is often true, extensive research and years of experience on the part of the manufacturer also back many well-known popular or supermarket brands.

## Therapeutic Diets

Often called prescription diets, these diets also are available through veterinarians for cats with

*The three basic types of cat food are canned, semimoist, and dry. Each type comes in a variety of flavors, so you should be able to find at least one that your cat enjoys.*

special needs. These foods are formulated and dispensed by veterinarians specifically for certain health conditions, such as heart disease, kidney disease, intestinal disorders, or obesity. While most of these special diets come in dry or canned form, at least one for recurrent gastrointestinal problems is available in semimoist form.

# Deciphering Cat Food Labels

Pet food companies are required by law to supply certain nutritional information on their labels. We have already discussed the life-cycle formulas and what these disclosures on a cat food label mean. A pet food label must also disclose whether the food is formulated to provide complete and balanced nutrition. The word *complete* means the food has all the necessary nutrients a cat needs for good health. The word *balanced* means those necessary nutrients are present in the proper proportions. If the label doesn't say the food is *complete* and *balanced,* chances are it isn't.

## Statement of Nutritional Adequacy

Pet food manufacturers must be able to prove that their products comply with nutritional guidelines set forth by the Association of American Feed Control Officials (AAFCO). They also must substantiate any claims they make that their product provides "100% complete and balanced" nutrition. To accomplish this, pet food manufacturers must either adhere to a proven formula or subject their products to lengthy feeding trials with live animals. Of the two, feeding trials offer more assurance that the food is adequately nutritious, because the product has been test fed to cats for a period of time under AAFCO protocols. Any product

that has undergone feeding trials says so on the package. Look for the company's statement of nutritional adequacy, which should say something similar to: *Animal feeding tests using AAFCO procedures substantiate that [this brand name] provides complete and balanced nutrition for the maintenance of adult cats.*

## Guaranteed Analysis

The required guaranteed analysis must state on the label only whether minimum or maximum amounts of nutrients, in percentages, were met. It doesn't have to list actual concentrations of specific nutrients. The problem with not knowing how much a product exceeds the minimum requirement for a certain nutrient, such as protein, is that sometimes too much can be just as bad as too little, depending on the cat's age and condition. What that means is that, while foods formulated for *all life stages of cats* are designed to meet normal nutritional needs of cats of all ages, some individuals, particularly older ones or those predisposed to certain health problems, may get far more of certain nutrients than they need.

## Ingredients List

Ingredients are supposed to be listed in descending order of predominance by weight, but this can be somewhat misleading: Meat may be listed first, leading the consumer to believe the product contains mostly meat, when in reality the summation of separately listed grains and cereals makes plant material the predominant ingredient. Some labeling terms are strictly regulated, while others are not. For example, the title wording of "Chicken for Cats," "Chicken Platter," "Chicken Entree," and others can have different meanings in terms of

the percentage of chicken the product must contain. A good way to check specific ingredient amounts is simply to call the manufacturer's toll-free number on the package and ask for the data. Many companies have consulting veterinarians and/or nutritionists, and you can judge for yourself how willing and able they

*(above left) If you don't want your cat to become a beggar, do not offer food directly from the table.*

*(left) Nursing moms need to eat a high quality, high protein growth and reproduction formula cat food to meet the nutritional demands of raising newborn kittens.*

*(above) Do not feed dog food to your cats because it does not contain enough protein, taurine, and other essential nutrients to promote good health in cats.*

seem to be to share information and answer your questions. A manufacturer's long-standing reputation can offer some assurance that correct product standards are met and maintained.

## Making Dietary Changes

With so many product lines and varieties to choose from, the important thing to remember is that no one perfect pet food exists for every cat and for every owner. That's why it may be necessary to change foods from time to time, as your cat's nutritional needs vary.

Although pet food labels provide helpful information, choosing a cat food solely by label contents or brand name is unwise. Instead, base your selection on how well your cat performs and maintains its overall condition on a particular food. Start with a high-quality kitten food that your breeder or veterinarian recommends. Then, during annual checkups, as your veterinarian assesses your cat's condition, remember to ask about your cat's changing dietary needs as it reaches adulthood and matures into middle and old age.

Make recommended changes to your cat's diet gradually, over a period of at least a week or more. Sudden changes in diet or feeding routine may result in symptoms of gastrointestinal upset in some animals, or your cat may simply refuse to eat the new food. So begin making any dietary change by mixing small amounts of the new food with your cat's current rations. Gradually increase the amount of new food as you decrease the amount of old food until the changeover is complete.

*Cats get fat for the same reasons people do: too much food and too little exercise.*

## Feeding Guidelines

As a guide to daily rations, follow the feeding instructions on the package and measure out the recommended portions. Keep in mind, however, that the product feeding guidelines provided on pet food packages are based on average nutritional needs and, therefore, are not intended as absolute amounts. Some individual cats may need greater portions, some less.

Most adult cats look forward to at least two meals a day, one in the morning and one in the evening. Others thrive on a canned food breakfast, supplemented with ample dry food left out for free-choice nibbling. Whatever routine works best for you and your pet, your cat will feel more secure if you feed it at the same time and in the same place each day.

# Homemade Diets

Because we humans tend to view food as a symbolic love offering, many owners like to express their affection for their cats by preparing home-cooked meals and snacks for them. But constructing a complete and balanced meal for a cat from scratch is not as easy as it sounds. It is a chore best left to the experts. That's because cats are carnivores by nature, which means they must have protein from animal sources to stay healthy. They cannot adapt safely to a vegetarian diet, nor can they thrive solely on "people food." Their nutritional needs are significantly different from those of humans, dogs, and other mammals.

One amino acid in particular, taurine, is indispensable, because the cat cannot manufacture this essential ingredient on its own. Research has shown that if a cat's food is taurine deficient, the animal stands a greater risk of developing blindness or a heart muscle disease called *dilated cardiomyopathy*. Prompted by such findings, manufacturers began routinely adding taurine to their commercial cat food products in the late 1980s, and since then, reported cases of dilated cardiomyopathy have declined dramatically.

Because the feline diet requires a delicate balance of numerous ingredients to maintain proper body functions and cell growth, too much or too little can be harmful. For this reason, home-cooked diets should be fed only in rare situations, such as when a cat is suspected of being allergic to an ingredient common in commercially prepared foods. Even then, the makeup of any routine homemade feline diet requires close supervision by a veterinarian with some expertise in animal nutrition.

This does not mean, however, that your cat is barred from ever sampling your home cooking or from tasting any tidbits of people food. On the contrary, such treats are okay on occasion, as long as you don't overdo it. Just keep the portions small, and don't make such offerings a daily habit, or your cat may begin turning up its nose at its own food. Remember, table scraps and people foods do not provide a complete and balanced diet for cats.

Also, garbage is garbage, so *never* feed your cat scraps that you would not eat, and do not feed bones, as these may splinter and lodge in your cat's throat or puncture parts of the digestive tract, leading to life-threatening complications.

# Obesity in Cats

If you're not careful, offering too many treats or too much people food can result in a fat cat. Obesity is probably the most common nutritional disorder among pets in the United States today. Moderately active or sedate cats that live in apartments and have little opportunity to exercise seem especially prone to developing this health disorder. But any cat, regardless of breed, can become fat if consistently overfed.

As in humans, obesity in cats can pose some serious health risks. The extra weight puts a strain on all organ systems and contributes to a shortened life span—and an overweight cat is a greater surgical and anesthetic risk.

The best way to judge whether a cat is overweight or underweight is to visually assess its body condition. This is not as easy as it sounds, however, because *ideal* weight varies from one individual to another, depending on a cat's age, sex, and other factors. In general, a cat is too fat if you cannot feel its ribs without having to probe with your fingers through thick, fleshy layers. Fat cats also often have sagging, pendulous bellies, bulges around the neck, and heavy accumulations of fat at the base of the tail. If you're unsure whether your cat is at ideal weight, simply ask your veterinarian during your cat's annual checkup.

## Overfeeding

Cats become fat for the same reasons that humans do—too many calories and too little exercise. While many cats with free access to food self-regulate their consumption appropriately, others overeat out of boredom. For this reason, when feeding dry food free choice, it is often best to measure and leave out only the recommended amount per day or per meal, depending on your feeding routine. Check the product's feeding guidelines for recommended amounts, and adjust the portions as needed to help your cat maintain its ideal body condition. Owners can unwittingly contribute to the problem of overeating by leaving out huge amounts of dry food that could last for days, instead of offering controlled portions to a cat that tends to overeat. If you choose to bulk feed your cat with a self-feeder—a practice that many owners find convenient—take time to observe your cat's eating habits and monitor its weight. Many cats self-fed in this manner will nibble a dozen tiny meals a day and stay fit and trim, while others will binge, overeat, and grow fat. If your cat turns out to be among the latter, you will have to stick with feeding controlled portions.

*Many cat owners find self-feeders and self-watering containers handy for dispensing food and water. If your cat tends to overeat, only offer controlled portions.*

## Snacks

Many owners enhance their cats' waistlines by offering too many high-fat, high-calorie gourmet snacks between meals. This situation is quite common, because so many people associate love and affection with offering food. While there's nothing wrong with offering your cat an occasional treat, remember not to overdo it. Also, don't substitute foods intended as treats for your cat's regular daily rations. Many commercial cat treats sold in stores are not labeled as *complete and balanced*. That's because they don't have to be, when they are intended only for intermittent use, and not for daily rations.

## Competitive Feeding

Some overweight cases may result from feeding cats together, which encourages competition. In addition, many cats tend to gain weight as they grow older, simply because they play less and need fewer calories.

## Medical Conditions

Weight gain and weight loss also can be symptoms of serious underlying medical conditions, such as diabetes, thyroid disorders,

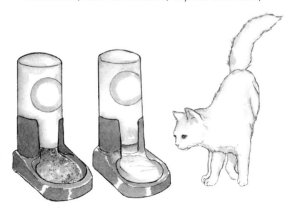

and kidney disease. Therefore, a veterinary examination is in order before you reduce your cat's feed or attempt to put it on any special diet.

## Weight Loss Diets

If you suspect that your cat is too fat, consult your veterinarian first, before you try to change the animal's diet. Your veterinarian can recommend an appropriate weight loss method to suit your animal's individual circumstances. Some veterinarians prefer to use a good therapeutic weight-reduction diet, while others recommend continuing on the customary food, but cutting down on portions and eliminating all snacks.

Therapeutic weight-reduction diets are nutritionally balanced but lower in calories

*If one of your cats requires a special diet, you may have to feed your cats individually.*

to produce weight loss without creating other deficiencies. They are also higher in fiber to promote a feeling of fullness in the animal. If your veterinarian recommends a therapeutic diet, and you have more than one cat, you may have to feed the one on the special diet separately.

Whatever method is used to achieve feline weight loss, owner compliance is the key to its success. It's also important that any weight loss be gradual and that changes in diet or food portions also be accomplished gradually, over a one- to two-week period. Putting an overweight cat on a crash or starvation diet can

*Always provide a daily source of fresh water for your cat to drink at will.*

result in a serious, potentially life-threatening liver disorder, called *hepatic lipidosis*.

# Foods to Avoid

## Dog Food

Commercial canine foods do not contain proper amounts of protein, taurine, and certain other nutrients to promote good health in cats. In other words, dog foods are for dogs; cat foods are for cats. If you have a dog and a cat, provide each with the appropriate food and, if they steal each other's food, feed them in separate locations.

## Supplements

Vitamin and mineral supplements, unless specifically recommended by a veterinarian, are not necessary when you feed your cat a high-quality, nutritionally complete and balanced commercial cat food. To compensate for nutrient losses during processing, pet food manufacturers add vitamins and minerals to their formulas to supplement natural nutrients contained in the primary ingredients. So, if you add more through additional supplementation (unless necessary to treat a specific condition), the balanced proportions of certain nutrients that your cat is receiving in its food could actually become unbalanced.

## Raw Foods

Do not feed raw meats, raw fish, raw liver, or raw egg whites. Meat alone is not a balanced meal and, if served raw, may contain harmful bacteria and parasites, including the organism that causes *toxoplasmosis* (see page 35). Raw fish can cause a thiamine deficiency. Raw liver, if fed daily in large quantities, can cause vitamin A toxicity. Raw egg whites have an enzyme that can interfere with vitamin biotin absorption. An occasional cooked whole egg is okay and good for the hair coat, as long as the egg is well done.

## Chocolate

While safe and delicious for humans, chocolate can be toxic to cats and dogs; therefore, keep candies, desserts, and baking chocolate covered and out of reach.

## Alcohol

Beer, wine, champagne, and liquor are all toxic to felines, even in small amounts. So, never, *never* let anyone give your cat an alcoholic beverage. Some people think it's funny to watch a cat lap up a little beer, then see it stagger in drunken circles. This practice is cruel and dangerous, because a cat's smaller body mass cannot adequately absorb alcohol's toxic effects. Just a little "hair of the dog" can turn deadly and fatally affect an animal's breathing.

# Diet and Urinary Tract Health

Over the years, numerous dietary elements have been blamed for causing the tiny *struvite* mineral crystals that can plug the feline urethra in FUS, a potentially life-threatening disease. (Some veterinarians refer to FUS as LUTD or FLUTD, for *feline lower urinary tract disease,* an umbrella term used to describe all disorders of the lower urinary tract.) The suspect list has included ash, magnesium, phosphorous, and calcium, among others. As each suspect ingredient was incriminated, major cat food manufacturers promptly reformulated their foods to reflect prevailing scientific research and to allay consumer concerns.

Current findings suggest that the overall mineral composition of cat food, rather than an excess of any single ingredient, determines whether the urine pH becomes too alkaline (too high), providing favorable conditions for crystals to form in the urinary tract. Magnesium content remains a secondary concern, enough to warrant restricting dietary levels when managing FUS. Reflecting this knowledge, specialty foods began to proliferate the market bearing label claims of *low magnesium, reduces urinary pH,* or *helps maintain urinary tract health.* Beyond these permissible statements, cat food manufacturers cannot claim that their products treat or prevent FUS, or any other disease, without approval from the Food and Drug Administration, because to do so would be touting the diet as a drug.

Today, most regular cat foods now on the market contain enough acidifying ingredients to help keep urine pH within safely acidic ranges. An acid urine helps dissolve struvite crystals or prevents them from forming in the first place, and researchers have noted a decrease in struvite stones, along with an increase in similar stones composed of calcium oxalate. The obvious conclusion is that the recomposition of commercial diets fed to cats is at least partly responsible for both changes.

While studies clearly suggest that restricting magnesium and maintaining a slightly acidic urine may help prevent struvite-related ure-thral obstructions, such a diet is certainly not considered a cure-all for *all* cats, particu-larly if it has the potential to cause other prob-lems. What this means is that, while the link between diet and urinary tract disease remains under investigation, the best advice is simply to consult your veterinarian before starting your cat on any special diet.

Furthermore, if you suspect your cat may have a urinary tract problem, seek veterinary attention immediately. Depending on the con-dition's severity, delaying medical treatment may result in a complete urethral blockage, leading to kidney damage or even death.

Symptoms of FUS include sudden changes in litter box habits, such as straining to urinate, urinating more often, passing bloody urine, or urinating in unusual places. Necessary treat-ment may include drugs combined with long-term dietary management.

## Don't Forget Water

Water has been called the "forgotten nutri-ent" because its importance is often down-played when discussing the proper feeding and care of cats; however, keeping fresh water in a clean bowl available for your cat at all times is a must. Cats can concentrate their urine and conserve water when necessary, but like most other mammals, they cannot survive for very long periods without water.

Milk is no substitute for water, nor is it a complete and balanced diet for adult cats. Some adult cats, like some people, develop a lactose intolerance to milk and will suffer from diarrhea if they drink it. Milk is useful as a temporary supplement for newly weaned kit-tens. When offering milk as a supplement, use a canned kitten milk replacer (available through veterinarians or pet shops) or a half-and-half mixture of evaporated milk and warm water, but avoid homogenized cow's milk.

# KEEPING YOUR MIXED BREED HEALTHY

## Visiting the Veterinarian

When you first get your cat, you'll want to have it checked out by a veterinarian within a week or two of bringing the animal home. During your cat's first visit to the veterinarian, discuss the need for any blood work or other tests to determine the status of your new cat's health. If you have other cats at home, you will want to have the new cat tested for feline leukemia virus (FeLV) and feline immunodeficiency virus (FIV) before exposing it to your other pets.

You also should request a stool analysis to rule out the presence of internal parasites (see chart on page 58). An infected queen can pass certain worms to her kittens through the placenta and through the breast milk. If the examination reveals parasites, your veterinarian will recommend appropriate treatment. Because deworming agents can cause toxic reactions, these drugs should be administered only under veterinary supervision. An effective parasite prevention program includes keeping cats indoors, maintaining good sanitation, and controlling fleas, rodents, and other vermin.

*During self-grooming, cats can swallow a lot of loose hair, which may accumulate into a hair ball inside the stomach.*

## An Ounce of Prevention

Getting annual veterinary checkups for your cat and adhering to a routine vaccination schedule are two ways to benefit both your cat and your pocketbook. Your cat will have a better opportunity to enjoy a longer, healthier life, and you can save money by preventing problems instead of treating them. The cost of aggressively treating a single serious illness can quickly surpass the money you spend on yearly physicals and routine booster shots throughout your cat's lifetime.

Keeping your cat indoors is probably the least expensive preventive health care measure you can provide your new feline companion, as an indoor cat is less likely to contract an illness from a free-roaming animal or to fall victim to other outdoor hazards. Having your cat spayed or neutered also benefits your cat's health—and your pocketbook—by reducing the animal's urge to roam and fight over mates, and by eliminating disease occurrence in the reproductive organs that are removed.

## Signs of Illness

With proper nutrition, regular veterinary checkups, good dental care, and routine vaccinations, you can reasonably expect your cat to live an average of 10 to 15 years. When illness

## Feline Diseases

| Disease | Symptoms | Prognosis |
|---|---|---|
| **Feline Viral Rhinotracheitis (FVR)** Highly contagious respiratory ailment caused by herpes virus; core vaccine is preventive | Sneezing; nasal discharge; crusty, watering eyes; appetite loss; lethargy | High mortality rate; survivors may become chronic carriers and shed virus during stress |
| **Feline Calicivirus (FCV)** Serious upper respiratory infection; core vaccine is preventive | Similar to FVR, with painful tongue, mouth ulcers, sore muscles, stiff gait, limping | May progress to pneumonia; survivors may become carriers |
| **Feline Panleukopenia Virus (FPV)** Also called feline distemper, feline parvovirus (unrelated to canine parvovirus), or feline infectious enteritis; core vaccine is preventive | Appetite loss, fever, depression, vomiting yellow bile, painful abdomen, low white cell count (leukopenia) | Often fatal, highly contagious among cats |
| **Feline Chlamydiosis** Respiratory infection, also called feline pneumonitis; noncore vaccine | Similar to FVR and FCV with weepy eyes, swollen eyelids | Quite contagious, especially among kittens |
| **Rabies** Core vaccine is preventive and required by law in many localities | Personality changes; irritability; paralysis facial, throat muscles; thick, stringy saliva | Fatal; transmissible to to humans and other mammals from infected animal's saliva via bite, open wound, or scrape |

does strike, however, you as the owner must be prepared to recognize the signs and symptoms and seek veterinary care right away. By recognizing a problem early and seeking treatment, you can greatly improve your cat's chances of a full recovery.

## Changes in Appetite

Often, the first telltale sign that something is wrong is a sudden change in appetite; therefore, any marked change in normal eating habits should be regarded with suspicion and carefully watched. If the problem doesn't

resolve itself quickly, within 24 hours or so, report your observations to a veterinarian.

## Changes in Litter Box Habits

Sudden changes in toilet habits also should be investigated for medical causes. If you notice that your cat is missing the litter box, straining to urinate, urinating more often, crying while trying to urinate, passing bloody urine, or urinating in unusual places, suspect a lower urinary tract infection or blockage and seek medical attention right away (see page 50 for more information about urinary tract health).

## Feline Diseases (continued)

| Disease | Symptoms | Prognosis |
|---------|----------|-----------|
| **Feline Leukemia Virus (FeLV)** Noncore vaccine is preventive; testing recommended to determine positive or negative status | Weight loss, anemia, poor appetite, lethargy, recurring infections | Often fatal, but infected cats may survive several years; impaired immune system may lead to cancers, secondary ailments |
| **Feline Infectious Peritonitis (FIP)** If exposure risk is high, noncore "nose drop" vaccine recommended | Fever, lethargy, appetite and weight loss, labored breathing, swollen belly | Potentially fatal; may affect internal organs; poses greatest hazard in multicat households |
| **Feline Immunodeficiency Virus (FIV)** Also called feline AIDS, cannot be transmitted to humans; keeping cats indoors is preventive | Lethargy, weight loss, gum disease, chronic infections, weakened immune system | No current cure or vaccine; testing recommended to determine status; virus spreads among cats through bites |
| **Feline Lower Urinary Tract Disease (FLUTD)** Also called feline urologic syndrome or FUS, caused by mineral crystals forming in the urethra; more common in male cats | Urinating often, straining to urinate, passing blood in urine, urinating in unusual places | May lead to urinary blockage, kidney damage, and death if left untreated; may require lifelong dietary management; recurrences are common |

## Other Trouble Signs

General signs of illness in the cat include lack of appetite, lethargy, and sometimes fever. Signs of respiratory diseases may include difficulty breathing, open-mouth breathing, coughing, or persistent sneezing with discharge from the nose and eyes. Digestive upsets and feline distemper may cause vomiting, diarrhea (with or without blood in the stool), and depression. Frequent vomiting and recurrent diarrhea may also indicate an intestinal infection caused by parasites.

In addition, take your cat to a veterinarian whenever you notice any of the following symptoms:

✔ unexplained or rapid weight loss
✔ increased thirst
✔ bleeding
✔ staggering
✔ panting
✔ lameness
✔ hair coat changes
✔ bloody stool
✔ persistent scratching
✔ excessive licking
✔ patchy hair loss
✔ crouching in a hunched-up position
✔ hiding in unusual places

Be on the lookout, too, for unusual lumps or swellings, which may indicate tumors, abscesses, or traumatic injury. This list is by no means complete. Because cats can succumb rapidly to illness, don't delay in seeking veterinary help at the first hint of trouble.

# How Vaccines Work

Several infectious diseases common in cats are caused by airborne organisms that can waft into your home on a breeze through open doors and windows. Even your hands, shoes, and clothing can serve as transmission modes, silently tracking in deadly disease-causing organisms. Fortunately, there are highly effective vaccines that combat many feline diseases, and that's why it's important to keep recommended vaccinations current, even if your cat stays inside all the time.

Vaccines artificially induce active immunity by stimulating the production of antibodies against a specific organism. As long as the antibody level remains high enough in the

*When you get a new cat, take it to your veterinarian for a thorough health exam and parasite check before introducing it to your other pets.*

body, the antibodies can attack and overcome a disease organism that attempts to invade. But because this protection wanes over time, your cat needs periodic boosters throughout its lifetime to maintain an adequate level of antibody in the system.

## Passive Immunity

Kittens acquire maternal antibodies from their mother's first milk, the *colostrum*. This is called *passive immunity*, and how long it lasts depends upon the antibody level in the mother's blood when the kittens are born. Protection usually lasts from 12 to 16 weeks, but it may wear off as early as eight weeks. Because kittens are highly susceptible to certain infectious diseases, vaccination at about eight weeks is recommended to ensure that they remain protected. However, if maternal antibodies are still present in the kitten's system when it receives its first vaccinations, those passive antibodies may render the vaccines ineffective. That's why vaccinations for the common feline respiratory infections and feline distemper are repeated at about 12 weeks of age, to ensure that they "take," as well as to provide the kitten with continuous immunity as maternal antibodies wear off.

## Boosters

Traditionally, veterinarians have given yearly boosters to maintain adequate immunity, but recent studies suggest that immunity with certain vaccines may last much longer than once thought. This new knowledge, combined with heightened concerns about soft-tissue tumors occurring at common vaccination sites (see page 59), prompted some practitioners to revisit their views on vaccine protocol.

In 1997 an advisory panel established by the American Association of Feline Practitioners and the Academy of Feline Medicine studied the issue and set new guidelines, separating vaccines into *core* and *noncore* categories and recommending less frequent boosters for the core diseases, since immunity appears to last longer.

## Vaccination Schedule

**Core vaccines** protect against severe or easily transmitted diseases and are recommended for *all* cats. The core diseases include rabies, feline distemper, and two upper respiratory illnesses, rhinotracheitis and calicivirus. Except for rabies, the core vaccines are typically combined into one convenient injection, to spare your cat the discomfort of multiple needle pricks. According to the new guidelines, most cats should get core vaccine boosters once every three years. However, cats with a greater risk of exposure—those allowed outdoors, used for breeding, or frequently exposed to other cats, for example—may still need booster shots once a year, or as recommended by your veterinarian. In addition, state laws dictate the frequency of rabies vaccinations and should be followed accordingly.

**Noncore vaccines** are recommended for cats at highest risk of exposure to feline leukemia virus (FeLV), feline infectious peritonitis (FIP),

*Your veterinarian will recommend an appropriate vaccination schedule for your cat.*

chlamydia (feline pneumonitis), and ringworm. These vaccines are considered optional and should be administered based on the risk of exposure. For example, a cat kept indoors has less chance of exposure to FeLV. However, a cat that goes outdoors, is frequently boarded or shown, has contact with other cats, or lives with a FeLV-positive cat has a greater chance of contracting the disease and needs the vaccine's protection. In addition, yearly boostering for cats receiving this protection is still recommended.

## Establishing Initial Immunity

Most experts still agree that the *ideal* immunization schedule begins with giving kittens their first combination core vaccination for upper respiratory infections and feline distemper at approximately six to eight weeks of age. Between eight and twelve weeks, the first in a series of two vaccinations for feline leukemia virus (FeLV) may be given. At twelve weeks,

## Internal Parasites

| | Symptoms | Mode of Transmission |
|---|---|---|
| **Tapeworms** Appropriate flea control measures are preventive | Fresh segments passed in stool look like white, wriggling grains of rice | Rodents and fleas; cats ingest fleas during self-grooming; larvae mature inside cat's intestines |
| **Roundworms** | Vomiting; diarrhea; weight loss; potbelly; overall poor condition; white, spaghettilike strands may be visible in vomit or stool | Contact with contaminated cat feces; kittens may contract from infected mothers |
| **Hookworms** | Anemia; diarrhea; weight loss; black, tarry stools | Larvae-infested soil; more prevalent in hot, humid areas |
| **Heartworms** Preventive medication recommended in high-risk regions | Shortness of breath, coughing, periodic vomiting | Mosquito bites; more prevalent in humid, mosquito-plagued regions |
| **Lungworms** | Dry, persistent cough | Contact with infected cats; eating infected birds or rodents |
| **Giardia** A protozoan parasite that causes an intestinal infection, giardiasis, in adult cats | Recurrent diarrhea; stools may be yellowish and foamy, often varying from soft to normal; overall unthrifty appearance | Drinking water that has been contaminated with fecal matter containing the organism's cysts |

another vaccination for upper respiratory infections and distemper is administered. Then, between twelve and sixteen weeks, kittens get a rabies vaccination, plus the second injection in the FeLV series. A year later, all vaccinations should be repeated, and thereafter followed up with periodic boosters on a schedule recommended by your veterinarian. Keep in mind that these time frames are generalizations that sometimes need to be adjusted to meet the individual needs of an orphaned or stressed kitten, for example. Your veterinarian may recommend a different vaccination schedule that is equally appropriate, depending on the region where you live and on your cat's current health status.

## Vaccine Reactions

Although side effects from vaccines are minimal, some cats do experience a brief period of mild lethargy after receiving their vaccinations, particularly the FeLV (feline leukemia virus). On rare occasions, some vaccine reactions can be serious, causing convulsions, labored breathing, and even death.

## External Parasites

| | Symptoms | Mode of Transmission |
|---|---|---|
| **Fleas** Even indoor cats are commonly plagued by these tiny, biting insects that feed on blood | Excessive scratching, presence of flea dirt (tiny black specks of flea excrement that turn bloody when dampened) in fur | Effective one-spot, once-a-month flea-control medications are available through veterinarians |
| **Ticks** Some ticks carry Lyme disease, which humans can catch | Felt as a bump in the cat's fur after tick burrows head into skin and swells from sucking blood | Remove tick promptly by grasping and pulling straight out with tweezers (wear rubber gloves) |
| **Lice** Uncommon in well-kept, healthy cats | White specks (nits) stuck to fur | Clip coat and bathe cat with medicated shampoo available through veterinarians |
| **Mites** Most common variety found in the cat is the ear mite, which burrows in the ear canal and can cause ear infection | Itchiness; hair loss; crusty sores; scaly dandruff; body odor; ear mites: crumbly, waxy, brown buildup in ears; head shaking; scratching at ears; holding ears to side of head; staggering | Veterinarian must identify specific mite variety before dispensing appropriate medication; other cats and dogs in household may require treatment also, due to contagion |
| **Ringworm** Not a worm at all but a fungus; prompt treatment required, as infection can spread from cats to humans | Itchiness; scaly skin; patchy hair loss | Clip coat; bathe cat; disinfect pet bedding; administer medications as recommended by a veterinarian; a noncore vaccine is preventive in high-risk households where ringworm has been a past problem |

Recent research also has raised concerns about a low incidence of tumors, called fibrosarcomas, developing at the injection sites of FeLV and rabies vaccines. While not caused by the vaccines directly, the tumors appear to result from a profound localized inflammation some cats experience, perhaps in reaction to the aluminum compounds used in the vaccine suspension.

As the matter remains under investigation, more veterinarians are recommending FeLV vaccination *only* for cats at greatest risk of contracting the disease, which is why the vaccine is considered noncore, or optional. Cats allowed outdoors or frequently exposed to other cats have the highest risk of FeLV exposure and certainly should be vaccinated. Also, veterinarians avoid giving the FeLV vaccine between the

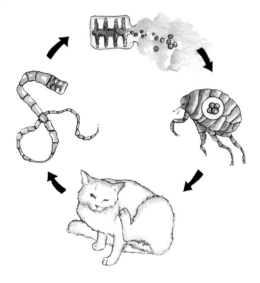

*Fleas can carry tapeworm larvae, which your cat may ingest as it grooms itself. The larvae grow into long, segmented strands within a cat's intestines. Some segments break off and are eliminated in the feces, where they often look like tiny wriggling grains of white rice.*

## Allergic Conditions

Like people, cats can be allergic to a host of things in their environment. Cats can develop allergies to pollen, weeds, grasses, mold spores, house dust, feathers, wool, insect stings, drugs, chemicals, and food ingredients. Instead of sneezing, watery eyes, and runny noses, however, cats' symptoms more likely involve itchy skin, face, and ears. Typical warning signs include compulsive rubbing against furniture or carpet and excessive scratching, licking, or chewing at itchy places. Gastrointestinal symptoms like vomiting and diarrhea also can occur, particularly if the allergen, or allergy-causing substance, is ingested in a food or drug. Redness, crusty skin, and hair loss around the nose, mouth, and face suggest a food allergy, or possibly an allergy to plastic feeding dishes. In the latter case, replacing plastic dishes with lead-free ceramic or stainless steel ones offers an easy remedy.

Unfortunately, most allergy cases are not so simple. Testing exists, but allergies remain difficult to diagnose. Treatment varies widely from patient to patient, depending on the cause and symptoms, and may include antihistamines or allergy shots. Recovery can take a long time,

shoulder blades because the tumors are less operable there. As part of an effort to standardize vaccine sites, and thus help track adverse reactions, the FeLV vaccine is now generally given in the cat's left rear leg, while the rabies shot is given in the right rear leg.

*Excessive scratching may be a sign that your cat has fleas.*

*Dental care is important for cats, too. Your veterinarian will show you how to brush your cat's teeth and recommend periodic dental cleanings.*

and because allergies usually persist for a lifetime, owners must commit to avoiding or reducing the allergen in the cat's environment for as long as the animal lives.

## Flea Allergy Dermatitis

Fleas cause the most common allergy condition seen in the cat, and even indoor cats are not immune. Following the mere scent of a warm-blooded animal, these tiny but relentlessly bloodthirsty and biting insects can jump through holes in walls or window screens, or ride in on a person's clothing or shoes in search of a suitable host. Once indoors, fleas lay eggs on the host and turn your cat's fur into a virtual nursery for millions more. As the cat moves and scratches, the eggs fall off into your carpets, upholstery, and bedding, where they hatch and begin the cycle anew.

Some cats are so allergic to flea saliva that the bite from a single flea will send them into a frenzy, scratching, biting, and licking to get at the culprit. The severe itching lasts long after the flea feeds and departs, so you may never even notice one of these nasty parasites on your pet.

The unsightly skin condition that results, called *flea allergy dermatitis,* is characterized by itchiness, hair loss, patchy redness (called "hot spots"), and scabby, crusty sores on the skin. Appropriate medications dispensed by

*A thorough veterinary checkup includes a look in the mouth to assess the condition of teeth and gums.*

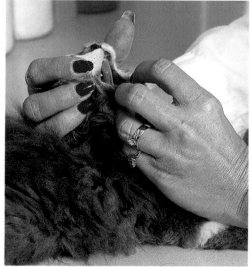

your veterinarian to relieve symptoms and diligent flea control measures help lessen the condition's severity and occurrence.

Effective flea control used to require an expensive arsenal of products designed to treat the pet and its environment at various phases of the flea's complex life cycle. This arsenal included sprays, dips, powders, flea collars, medicated shampoos, and room foggers, all targeted to kill or control fleas at the egg, larval, pupal, or adult stages. Often, these products failed to be effective when applied during the wrong life cycle of the insect and required repeating. They could also be potentially dangerous if used inappropriately or in combination with incompatible products, and some products are especially dangerous if used on too-young kittens or on sick, debilitated cats. Even flea collars, although easy to use, posed a risk of strangling or choking, unless designed with elastic or breakaway sections to make them safer. In recent years, however, the introduction of oral and topical once-a-month flea control products for cats has made effective flea control much easier. Ask your veterinarian about these convenient and highly effective products.

# Dental Care

Cats are not prone to cavities, but they are susceptible to gum disease, which can eventually lead to tooth loss. Dental disease can also silently compromise your cat's immune system and overall health by allowing bacteria to leak into the bloodstream from pockets of pus around sore, infected gums. Normal, healthy gums are pink, but diseased gums are tender, red, and swollen—signs of gingivitis (inflamed gums) caused by plaque and tartar buildup.

Left untreated, this condition causes the gums to recede gradually and the teeth to loosen. Bad breath is a cardinal sign of dental disease. A cat with dental problems may also have difficulty eating because its teeth and gums hurt, and as a result may lose weight and condition.

The best way to prevent such problems is to regularly brush or rinse your cat's teeth with oral hygiene products designed for use in animals. Your veterinarian can recommend an appropriate mouth rinse or a non-foaming, enzymatic toothpaste made especially for animals and demonstrate the proper use of these products. Animal toothpastes, which come in fish, poultry, and malt flavors for cats, are designed to dissolve plaque without a lot of scrubbing action.

**Warning:** *Never* use human toothpastes, because they will burn the back of your cat's throat and, if swallowed, can cause stomach upset.

From time to time, you may need to have your cat's teeth professionally cleaned. For this procedure, the cat is anesthetized, and the veterinarian uses an ultrasonic scaler to blast away the ugly, brown tartar and polish the teeth.

# Medicating Your Cat

Getting your cat used to having its mouth opened and handled will make it much easier for you to give it oral medications, should the need arise. Otherwise, the ordeal is likely to be a two-person job, with one person holding the cat while the other administers the medicine. Pills and liquids, covered here, are the most common forms of medication you will likely

*To give a cat a pill, grasp the head gently with one hand, placing your thumb and index finger on the cat's cheekbones. Tilt the head back slightly, then gently pry open the jaws with your other hand. Drop the pill as far back in the throat as possible. Then hold the cat's mouth shut and stroke its throat to encourage swallowing.*

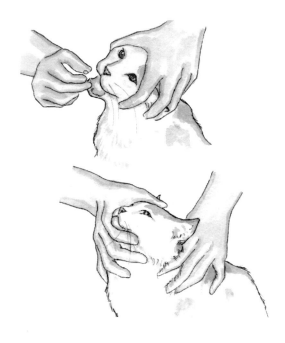

have to administer, but whether your cat's condition calls for oral medications, injections, eye ointments, eardrops, or force-feeding that you must do at home, ask your veterinarian to explain and demonstrate the best method of application. Make sure you understand how and when to administer any medication before you attempt to do it yourself, and know what to expect in terms of recovery time and side effects.

*Never* give your cat any drug or over-the-counter drugs or remedies meant for humans. Tylenol and similar products that contain an ingredient called *acetaminophen,* are especially deadly to cats, even in small amounts. Aspirin products can also be lethal to cats. While certain products made for humans can be used for cats, the dosage, in many cases, must be diluted or carefully controlled and monitored, so never try to medicate or treat your cat with any product that is not specifically labeled as *safe for use on cats* without seeking veterinary advice first.

## Pills

To restrain a struggling cat, wrap its entire body in a large towel, leaving only the head sticking out. To medicate, grasp the cat's head with your thumb and index finger on its

cheekbones and tilt back the head. With the forefinger of your other hand, gently pry open the jaws, then drop the pill as far back into the throat as possible. Hold the cat's mouth shut with one hand and stroke its throat with your other. The stroking motion encourages the cat to swallow.

## Liquids

To administer liquid medication, tilt the head back slightly, insert an eyedropper or syringe (without needle) into the corner of the mouth and gently squeeze in a few drops at a time, allowing the cat time to swallow. Do not squirt the medication into the cat's mouth too quickly or too forcefully, because the cat may accidentally inhale the liquid into the lungs. This could lead to pneumonia. Hold the animal's mouth

shut and stroke the throat until the cat swallows.

Some liquid medications can be mixed in the cat's food, if they are not too bitter tasting. Cats can easily detect medications added to their food and usually eat around the edges or refuse the food altogether. Sometimes, lacing the drug with tuna oil or concealing it in strong-smelling, fish-flavored canned food works. When adding medication to food, make sure your other animals do not consume it.

## Preventing Hair Balls

Hair balls are soft, tubular masses of ingested hair. Cats, especially longhaired ones, can swallow a lot of loose hair as they groom themselves, particularly at the height of shedding season. Normally, this creates no problem; the hair simply moves through the digestive

*Keeping cats healthy and free of fleas and other parasites helps safeguard your pets as well as your family.*

tract and gets eliminated the natural way. Occasionally, however, too much hair accumulates in the stomach and is vomited back up as a hairball. In more serious cases, the hair may form a large mass further along in the digestive tract, causing a blockage and requiring an enema or even surgery to remove. Signs of a blockage include refusal to eat or regurgitating food shortly after eating.

Regular grooming is the easiest and cheapest way to prevent hair balls. Brushing and combing your cat helps remove the loose, dead hair it would swallow otherwise.

If your cat makes a habit of spitting up hair balls on your carpets, several petrolatum-based

hair ball pastes are available through veterinarians or at pet supply stores. To administer one of these remedies, squeeze a ribbon of paste onto your finger and entice the cat to lick it, or place an amount on the cat's tongue or paw. Another option is to dab some plain petroleum jelly (Vaseline) on the top part of your cat's front paw to lick off. These products help lubricate the hair mass so that it expels more easily.

Grass also seems to act as a purgative to help cats expel excess hair from the stomach.

*Keep your cat from munching on your houseplants by providing it with a supply of grass.*

You can grow a fresh supply of grass indoors for your cat, and most pet stores sell kitty grass kits specifically for this purpose. Most cats love to nibble on greenery, and providing your cat with its own personal supply of grass may help keep it from grazing on your houseplants.

## Be Prepared

The key to successfully coping with any emergency is to be prepared for it. Always keep your veterinarian's emergency number handy. In addition, assemble the following items in a first aid kit:

✔ a blanket or towel to wrap your cat in for warmth and safe restraint

✔ gauze pads and strips for bandaging

✔ hydrogen peroxide antiseptic (it's fresh only if it bubbles) to clean wounds and induce vomiting

✔ antibiotic ointment, such as Neosporin, for superficial wounds

✔ tweezers, handy for removing foreign objects from paw pads, or from the throat if the cat is choking

✔ waterproof pouch to hold ice for controlling swelling and bleeding

✔ scissors and adhesive tape

✔ artificial tears or sterile saline eye rinse to flush foreign material from eyes

✔ rectal thermometer, pediatric size

## Be Observant

Cats often conceal illness or pain, but observant owners can detect subtle behavior changes that cue them that all is not well. Early injury and disease detection can greatly enhance the odds of full recovery. Set aside time once a week to assess your cat's overall condition. Make a practice of inspecting your cat for white teeth; pink gums; clean, pink ears; clear, bright eyes free of discharge; clean fur free of flea dirt; and a firm body free of lumps, bumps, and tender spots. By doing so regularly, you are more apt to notice anything out of the ordinary.

## Control Bleeding First

When a cat is injured and bleeding, it may go into shock from blood loss and die before you reach a veterinary clinic. To control bleeding, cover visible wounds with gauze pads or some clean material and apply gentle, direct pressure over the site for several minutes. Do not attempt to splint or straighten fractured limbs, as this could cause more damage.

## Transport Properly

Never pick up an injured animal by placing your hands under the belly. This will only worsen chest or abdominal injuries. If the cat is lying down, approach it from behind, slide one hand under the chest and one hand under the rump, and gently place it in a pet carrier or on a blanket for transport. If the cat is crouched, grasp the scruff of the neck with one hand, place the other hand under the hips and rear legs for support, and cradle the cat in your arms. If the cat struggles, wrap it in a large towel or blanket, leaving only the head sticking out. Remember, no matter how gentle your cat is, it may bite or claw you if it's in pain. Place an unconscious cat on its side for transport and cover it with a blanket to keep it warm.

## Accidental Poisoning

If you suspect your cat has ingested a potentially hazardous substance, call your veterinarian immediately. Do not induce vomiting unless an expert advises it. Some substances can cause more harm when vomited back up. When advised to induce vomiting, administer a small amount of hydrogen peroxide or warm salt water by mouth with an eyedropper. If you know what poisonous substance was

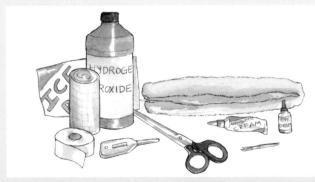

ingested, take the package or a sample with you to the veterinarian.

For 24-hour assistance, seven days a week, call the National Animal Poison Control Information Center, operated by the University of Illinois. The hotline number is (800) 548-2423. The service charges a flat fee for each initial case, payable by credit card, but follow-ups are free. Those with short questions and those not wanting to use credit cards may have a per-minute fee added to their telephone bill by calling (900) 680-0000.

Certain medications and flea products cause some cats to salivate a little immediately after application. In many cases, this is no cause for concern, and the reaction subsides after a minute or two. However, if your cat begins salivating *heavily* after you've applied a topical flea preparation to its fur, or if it staggers or shows other unusual signs, rinse the substance off right away and call your veterinarian. Don't use the product on your cat again. Remember, *never* use products not specifically labeled as safe for use on cats, and *never* use dog products on cats, as the ingredients may be too strong.

If your cat's coat or paws become contaminated by bleach, pesticides, paint products, household cleaners and disinfectants, oil, tar, antifreeze, or other potential poisons, wash off the offending substance immediately. If necessary, clip away the affected fur. If the coat appears to be heavily saturated, or if you believe the cat may have already licked some of the substance from its coat or paws, seek veterinary help.

### Removing Foreign Objects

If the cat is salivating, gagging and pawing at its mouth, it may be choking on a foreign object in its mouth. Frequent culprits are bones, toothpicks, or staples stuck between the upper back teeth. Cats in this predicament often become quite frantic and, in their frenzied state, may claw or bite anyone who tries to help them. Transporting the animal to a nearby veterinary clinic for emergency assistance is the best

*To safely restrain a struggling cat, wrap it in a blanket or large towel, leaving only the head sticking out. Transport carefully. Remember, an otherwise gentle, docile cat may bite or claw you if it is hurt or frightened.*

approach, but if the cat is your own, and you feel you can do so safely, you may want to try opening the mouth and gently pulling back the tongue for a better view down the throat. However, if the cat is a stray and unknown to you, *never* attempt to inspect the mouth or throat, due to the potential risk of rabies. If you can see an obstructing object in the mouth, use tweezers to gently extract it. If the object does not readily dislodge, make no further attempt to remove it without veterinary help. You may do more harm than good. Never poke tweezers into the eyes or ears; foreign objects lodged in these areas are best removed by a professional.

### Heatstroke and Frostbite

These conditions require immediate medical attention. To prevent frostbite, keep your cat indoors and avoid overexposure during cold weather. To prevent heatstroke, never leave your cat in a parked car, not even for a few minutes, not even with the windows cracked. Temperatures inside a car rapidly climb too high for safe tolerance, even on mild days. With only hot air to breathe, your cat can quickly suffer brain damage and die from heatstroke. Signs of heat stress include panting, vomiting, glazed eyes, rapid pulse, staggering, and red or purple tongue. Cool the body with tepid water, wrap in wet towels, and transport to a veterinary clinic immediately.

# UNDERSTANDING YOUR MIXED BREED

## How Cats Communicate

Cats have an extensive vocabulary of mews and meows, and some are more vocal than others. There are quiet, soft-spoken cats that seldom resort to "talking" unless doing so is absolutely necessary to make themselves understood, then there are the impish loudmouths who seem to relish the impact a well-timed, raucous, throaty howl has on the household in the middle of the night. Certain purebreds, such as the Siamese, are noted for their vocal qualities, but since a mixed breed is pot luck, you won't know what you're getting until your cat has had a chance to settle in for a while.

### Vocal Sounds

According to the intonation, a cat's meow can express many moods and needs. For example, a loud, throaty howl or an urgent yowl demands attention; they may mean that your cat is in distress, or that it simply wants something to eat. Queens in heat let out a particularly annoying mating call to the neighborhood toms that's loud and persistent enough to rattle the senses. Mother cats, on the other hand, chirp softly, in a most comforting and soothing way, when calling to their kittens.

*Cats use their bodies—a stance, a movement of the tail, the flip of an ear—to communicate with other cats and with humans.*

### Purring

The most universally recognized and beloved feline sound of all, the purr, is also the most mysterious. Experts still puzzle over the exact mechanism that causes or enables big cats and domestic cats alike to purr. Most scientists say the sound is probably produced by vibrations in the larynx, or voice box, as the cat breathes in and out. By whatever means, your cat can control and produce at will this most soothing of all feline sounds.

But *why* cats purr is really more mysterious than *how* they do it. Even kittens as young as two days old can purr, suggesting that the sound may be a special form of bonding between mother and offspring, the purpose of which may be to communicate and reassure that all is well in the nest. This theory seems plausible, given the fact that, for human caretakers, cuddling a purring cat can help relieve stress, promote a mutual sense of well-being, and strengthen the human/feline bond. Perhaps by purring in the presence of a caretaker, cats are responding as they would to a "parent cat," communicating that everything is okay.

Of course, there is a long-held belief that cats purr to express contentment, when they feel happy, secure, warm, and well fed. But they've also been known to purr when nervous (at the veterinarian's office), upset, sick, hurt, or hungry. Interestingly, cats have even been

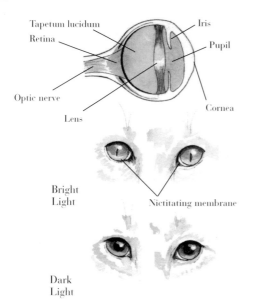

Tapetum lucidum
Retina
Iris
Pupil
Optic nerve
Cornea
Lens

Bright Light
Nictitating membrane

Dark Light

*A cat's eyes appear to glow in the dark because a special layer of cells in the eye, called the* **tapetum lucidum,** *acts like a mirror, reflecting all available light back onto the retina. This remarkable feature gives the cat its exceptional night vision.*

observed to purr as they lay dying. As a result, the generally accepted theory is that cats purr not only to express pleasure, but also to calm and comfort themselves when faced with an unpleasant situation.

### Body Language

The feline vocabulary involves more than just purring, mewing, and meowing. Cats let their elegant bodies do most of the talking, and they communicate eloquently with their feline and human companions alike. A particular body stance, a simple flick of the tail, or the flip of an ear all can have specific meaning. For example, when your cat greets you with ears pricked forward and tail held high, with just the tip slightly bending forward, he or she is saying, "Hello, old friend. I'm sure glad you're here!"

When confronted by a stranger or an adversary, however, a timid or submissive cat

crouches, lowers its ears, and drops its tail. A frightened or defensive cat can make itself appear as large as possible by arching its back and fluffing its fur out fully. An angry cat also crouches low, but its stance and tail action differ from that of the submissive cat. With ears flattened, muscles tense and ready to spring to action, the angry cat appears poised to attack. The flicking of its tail from side to side clearly signals a warning, "Back off!" If that posture fails to get the message across, a loud hiss or a low, drawn-out growl leaves no doubt that an attack is imminent.

## The Primary Senses

Much of the mystery associated with felines is a direct result of their unique anatomy, which endows them with their special nighttime hunting prowess. The cat's mastery of the night has sparked awe, envy, and fear in the human soul throughout the ages—enough, at various times in history, to elevate this superbly adapted nocturnal hunter to the status of a god or damn the entire species as devils.

A cat possesses five known senses, which are far superior to ours. Understanding how your cat perceives its world through these highly developed senses helps explain many feline behaviors that appear incomprehensible otherwise.

## Sight

As primarily nocturnal hunters, cats possess excellent night vision. Although they have poor color vision, cats can see much better in dim light than humans can, but they cannot see in total darkness. There must be some minimal light available for the feline eye to amplify. This ability stems from a special layer of cells behind the feline retina, called the *tapetum lucidum,* which makes a cat's eyes appear to glow in the dark. These specialized cells act like a mirror, reflecting all available light back onto the retina and giving the cat its exceptional ability to see well in low-light conditions.

The feline pupil can also dilate much wider than the human eye. This allows the cat's eye to collect light more effectively in dim conditions. A cat that feels threatened, frightened, or defensive will dilate its pupils to see better over a wider area. Of course, the cat's pupil works the other way, too. On sunny days, the pupils constrict to vertical slits to block out bright light.

Well suited to hunting and night stalking, a cat's eyes are especially adept at detecting the slightest movements made by small prey animals. Many prey animals have evolved with the instinct to "freeze" in place and remain perfectly still when they detect the scent or presence of a nearby predator. A stalking cat hard at work will crouch patiently for long periods, staring at nothing, or so it appears, until the concealed or camouflaged prey finally reveals its whereabouts with barely a twitch in the grass.

Another special characteristic of the cat's eye is an opaque third eyelid, called the nictitating membrane, which helps protect and lubricate the eyeball. Although usually not visible under normal conditions (except occasion-ally when the cat is sleeping), the third eyelid may protrude from the eye's inside corner if the eye gets injured, irritated, or infected. In addition, this white, filmy membrane is some-times more visible over the eyes with certain diseases and, therefore, warrants a veterinary examination if it persists beyond an occasional, sleepy blink.

## Smell

Cats possess an acute sense of smell, far superior to a human's sense of smell, but defi-nitely not as good as that of the dog. As with dogs and other animals, cats use odors and the sense of smell to identify each other as well as objects in their territory. For example, when two cats meet on friendly terms, they typically engage in a ritual of sniffing each other about the head and anal areas, where scent glands exude a vast databank of personal information. Among cats, this behavior is the equivalent of the human handshake and hello.

**Jacobson's organ:** As part of their sense of smell, cats and many other mammals have a special scent mechanism, called the vomero-nasal or Jacobson's organ. This specialized scent organ adds a different dimension to animals' ability to detect and identify odors and is believed to give mammals an edge on finding mates by helping them sort out sex-related scent hormones called pheromones.

Located in the roof of the mouth behind the incisor teeth, this special organ actually allows cats to taste odor molecules. When using the Jacobson's organ, a cat curls its upper lip back and, with teeth bared and mouth partially agape, sniffs the air deeply through both nose and mouth. This grimace, often mistaken for a silent growl or a snarl, is called the flehmen

*Due to specialized cells in the eye that reflect and magnify available light, the cat possesses excellent night vision, but it cannot see in total darkness.*

response. Like many animals, cats sometimes display flehmen when examining urine and scent marks left by other animals and during territorial or mating rituals.

## Taste

Specialized cells on your cat's tongue enable it to detect the chemical components of food as saliva dissolves them in the mouth. These taste buds send signals along nerve pathways to the brain, where taste identification actually takes place. The food with the greatest appeal to a carnivore's palate is, of course, meat. And being naturally evolved meat-eating predators, cats like their meals lukewarm, or as near the average body temperature of most small prey mammals as possible—not hot, and certainly not cold, as in straight out of the refrigerator.

Pet food industry taste preference tests suggest that cats can distinguish between salty or sour foods, but they cannot taste simple sugars. According to the experts, this means that cats generally should not prefer sweet or sugary foods, although we've all heard owners' tales to the contrary. But since many sweets are also high in fat, the cat with the sweet tooth is probably craving the yummy taste of the high-fat ingredients, and not the sugar.

*When a cat hears something of interest, it pricks or swivels its ears in that direction and focuses intently on the sound.*

*A balancing mechanism in the cat's inner ear enables the animal to right itself in midair during a fall. The cat rotates its head and shoulders first, followed by the hindquarters. Although cats usually manage to right themselves and land on all fours, injuries sustained from the impact are still common.*

## Touch

Your cat's whiskers are highly sensitive tactile organs, so *never* clip them. There's a common saying that if a cat's whiskers can pass through a small opening, the cat knows the rest of its body can fit through and follow. This may be more fancy than fact (especially since obesity is such a common problem among today's house cats); however, cats do use their whiskers to sense and avoid objects in dim light and to detect vibrations and changes in their environment. Cats also use their whiskers to touch and gauge the size of prey caught in their paws.

## Hearing

Few people are surprised to learn that cats can hear better than humans. Because their normal prey typically emits high-pitched sounds, cats' ears are tuned to frequencies well beyond the range of human hearing. Cats can also quickly learn to recognize the source and meaning of certain sounds; for example, chirping birds mean a possible meal is nearby. This associative ability extends from the hunting ground into the household, and after the first time or two, your cat will come running to the buzz of an electric can opener, the whisk of a pop-top lid, or the opening of the refrigerator door. And if you consistently call your cat by name at each feeding, it will quickly learn its name, and perhaps even come when called.

## A Sense of Balance

Besides their five primary senses, cats also possess an extraordinary sense of balance. If a cat rolls off a windowsill and falls in an upside-down position, a balance mechanism in the inner ear enables the cat to rotate its forequarters first, then the hindquarters, so that it automatically rights itself in midair and lands on all fours. This remarkable ability is known as the *righting reflex*. The cat's supple and flexible spine also contributes to its maneuverability in free-fall. Even with these impressive assets, however, cats that fall from great heights can still sustain fractures and other serious injuries. In fact, veterinarians see so many of these types of injuries that they've classified them under a special name—*high-rise syndrome*.

# Mating Habits

Even though you plan to spay or neuter your mixed-breed cat, it's still important to understand feline mating behaviors to fully appreciate the species. In the language of professional cat breeders, a breeding female cat is called a queen. An intact male is called a tom or stud. He reaches sexual maturity between nine and fourteen months. A queen may have her first heat cycle, called estrus, well before she is one year old and fully mature enough to have a healthy pregnancy. This is one reason why, when intact animals are allowed to roam freely and breed indiscriminately, many queens and kittens suffer and die needlessly. Spaying or neutering your queen or tom is a responsible, caring choice every mixed-breed cat owner should make to help alleviate this senseless suffering, especially if you plan to let your cat go outdoors.

## The Heat Cycle

A queen comes into heat according to seasonal rhythms, typically in early spring, midsummer, and early fall. Feline reproductive cycles appear to be influenced by lengthening daylight hours, which explains why cats in the Northern Hemisphere cycle opposite to those in the southern half of the world. Most queens have heat cycles every two or three weeks during the breeding seasons; others cycle only once a month, although there are many exceptions.

Usually, there's no mistaking when a queen comes into season, but some queens do have "silent" heats. The hallmark signs of this heightened period of sexual receptivity include increased restlessness and persistent vocal calling.

## Induced Ovulation

Female cats are unusual in that they, unlike most other mammals, do not ovulate spontaneously during their cycles. Instead, they are *induced ovulators,* meaning that the sex act must occur to induce the release of eggs from the ovaries. To help accomplish this, the male's penis is ridged with tiny spines or barbs that scrape the inside of the queen's vagina during copulation. This physical stimulation apparently sends a message along nerve pathways to areas in the brain that release luteinizing hormone, a chemical that prompts ovulation.

## Signs of Pregnancy

If the queen becomes pregnant, gestation normally lasts an average 65 or 66 days. About three weeks after conception, the queen's nipples redden, a condition breeders call *pinking up.* The queen's attitude may become more maternal and affectionate. Her appetite may increase, and she will gradually put on a few extra pounds. In about a month, her abdomen becomes noticeably swollen from the kittens growing inside her.

*A female cat in heat will naturally assume the lordotic position or mating stance when you stroke her back near the base of the tail.*

## Birth and Kitten Development

Born with eyes and ears closed, kittens are unable to see or hear at birth. Healthy ones begin suckling just minutes after birth. It is crucial for kittens to begin nursing soon after birth so they can ingest disease-fighting antibodies contained in the mother's first milk, called the colostrum. Kittens that do not receive this first milk are less likely to survive. During the first weeks, the queen stays with her kittens most of the time, nursing and cleaning them and keeping them warm. She also must lick their genital areas routinely to stimulate elimination, as newborn kittens cannot control these essential body functions on their own for the first few weeks of their lives.

In about 10 days, the kittens' eyes begin to open. At first, all kittens' eyes are blue, changing to their adult shade at about 12 weeks of age. By 15 to 20 days old, kittens start crawling; soon afterward, they begin to stand and toddle. At about four to six weeks, kittens can experiment with soft, solid foods, and gradual weaning may begin. Also by this time, they can control their own elimination, and litter box training can begin. At one month, kittens begin to play with each other, engaging in mock chase and combat games intended to hone their hunting skills. Between 8 and 16 weeks is generally the best time for them to leave their mothers and go to new homes.

# Sleeping Habits

Cats evolved primarily as nocturnal hunters, creatures on the prowl for prey at night. The successful deployment of their nighttime skills requires that they be well rested and in peak condition. As a result, insomnia is not a common problem among cats. They sleep throughout the day, often catnapping as much as 18 hours a day. By bedtime, their hunting instincts rev into high gear, and your toes wriggling under the bed covers present the perfect prey to pounce upon. This nocturnal tendency probably contributed to the time-honored tradition of "putting the cat out" at night, no doubt so that a weary owner could get some sleep.

Fortunately, indoor cats adapt readily to our diurnal timetables, and many sleep soundly all night on their owners' beds, doubling as failsafe alarm clocks come morning. As with people, cats that get plenty of exercise generally sleep better.

# Hunting Habits

To observe your cat's superb hunting prowess in action, simply entice the animal to play. Using an interactive toy, such as a kitty fishing pole with sparklers or feathers attached to the end of the line, slowly reel in your cat as it stalks the wriggling lure. Watch as your cat crouches and creeps forward silently, pupils wide and eyes fixed, watching for the slightest move that might mean the "prey" is going to run. Muscles remain tensed and ready for instant pursuit. The tail twitches in anticipation. As the cat prepares to pounce, it wriggles its rear end and treads quietly with the back legs, as if testing which foot will provide the better spring action. Before the feather flutters one last time, the cat springs on it with claws extended, the front paws striking in deadly accuracy to pinion the prey. One well-placed "death" bite with the powerful canine teeth ends the struggle.

# Territorial Marking

By nature, cats are highly territorial creatures and will readily notice any new objects or changes in their environment.

## Rubbing

This is one means by which cats mark objects in their environment and claim them as their territory. Your cat will, no doubt, endearingly and lovingly greet you by rubbing against your legs. Don't be fooled! The gesture is much more than a mere expression of affection. By rubbing against furniture and other objects, cats leave behind scent from glands around their faces, mouths, and tails. Humans can't smell the scent, but other cats can. The message means "I was here first, and this territory is mine!"

Cats will routinely travel the boundaries of their territory to inspect and refresh these scent markers. Your cat views you as an integral part of its territory, and each time it rubs against you, it is marking you with its scent and reaffirming "ownership." In addition, the mingling of your smell on the cat's fur helps identify you as a member within its circle of friends. So, when your cat rubs against your legs in greeting, it really is saying "I own you!"

## Spraying

Less endearing is the feline habit of spraying urine to mark territory. Although intact males are more prone to this behavior, females sometimes do it to communicate their reproductive status, especially when in heat. Spaying and neutering tend to curb this undesirable behavior, but both sexes, whether whole or altered, may occasionally resort to spraying when engaged in a dispute with another cat over territory or dominance. For this reason, the problem is more likely to occur in multicat households, particularly in overcrowded conditions.

## Clawing

When a cat scratches the arm of the couch, it is not misbehaving. Like spraying and rubbing, this action, too, is an instinctive territorial marking behavior. The cat is actually marking the scratched object with scent from glands in its paws. The cat is also fulfilling an instinctive need to keep its basic defense weaponry—its claws—sharp and trim. Similar to filing fingernails, the in-and-out action on wood, carpet, or rough fabric helps strip away the dead, outer layers of the claws.

*Whether your cat rubs against your leg or a leg of furniture, it is actually marking that object with scent from glands around its tail and face.*

*During mock play battles, kittens learn when to retract their claws so that they do not hurt each other.*

Outdoor cats can often be observed marking and sharpening their claws on the trunks of trees. For an indoor cat, this perfectly natural feline behavior can become a problem when the scent that's left behind on your furniture, combined with an apparent preference for the spot, continues to draw the cat back to the same site to claw until the couch arm becomes a shredded mess. A scratching post is a must for indoor cats in order to prevent destructive clawing.

# Destructive Clawing

You cannot eliminate the cat's instinctive need to claw, but you can modify and redirect the behavior by providing your cat with a suitable scratching post. Inappropriate clawing habits, once firmly established, can be difficult to break, so begin teaching your kitten to use a scratching post early, as soon as you bring it home.

### Vinyl Nail Caps

Once a destructive clawing habit becomes firmly entrenched, one humane alternative for dealing with the problem is to glue vinyl nail caps onto a cat's freshly trimmed claws. These caps, which can be purchased through veterinarians, give the nails a soft, blunt tip and help prevent snags in carpets, furniture, and drapes. The major drawback to this method is that the vinyl caps have to be reapplied every four to six weeks, as the nails grow. The application is simple, however, and owners can purchase take-home kits and learn to manicure their cats' nails themselves. Ask your veterinarian to

demonstrate the product. Vinyl nail caps are not recommended for outdoor animals because they inhibit a cat's ability to climb.

### Declawing

This surgical procedure is the least desirable alternative for dealing with destructive clawing and should be considered only as a last resort after other methods have failed. Banned in some countries, this controversial procedure is still performed in the United States by veterinarians who consider it a viable option over having to euthanatize the cat or surrender it to an animal shelter for adoption.

The declawing procedure involves putting the cat under anesthesia and surgically amputating the claw tip and the last bone of the toe. Generally, only the front claws are removed, because the hind feet are not used for scratching furniture. While this procedure may offer a permanent solution to destructive clawing problems, it is not painless. After the operation, the cat suffers some pain and risk of infection as its mutilated paws heal.

There are other drawbacks, too. With only the front claws removed, a cat still can use its rear claws to climb trees, but it just can't climb as well as before. The procedure clearly inhibits climbing and self-defense, which means that cats allowed to roam freely outdoors should not be declawed and disadvantaged in this way.

# House Soiling

Destructive clawing and house soiling are the two major behavior problems that often land many cats in animal shelters. This is why, when adopting an adult cat, you want to find out as much as you can about its history and about why it was surrendered in the first place. Once a bad habit becomes well established, it can be difficult, although not impossible, to break. But some owners either don't understand the motivating factors well enough to deal with them, or they simply give up too soon and give away the cat.

Understanding what is normal behavior for cats under natural conditions is crucial to understanding how to deal with them when things go wrong under confined conditions. For example, cats, being naturally territorial, mark and defend areas where they spend most of their time. As discussed, clawing and spraying are two means of marking territory. Knowing what motivates a certain behavior is the key to figuring out how to modify or correct it.

While spraying and litter box problems can occur in single-cat homes, they are more common in multicat households, particularly if you have too many cats crowded into too small an area. If you have more than one cat, you can help prevent elimination problems by providing each animal with its own litter box. Even then,

the more aggressive cat may sometimes chase another away from the litter box. If this happens, place the boxes in separate rooms or at opposite ends of the house, to give each cat a sense of privacy and individual territory.

Generally, when a housebroken cat eliminates outside its litter box, it is either marking territory or displaying a preference for a particular spot, surface, or litter box filler. Contrary to popular belief, cats do not begin house soiling out of spite. At least, that's what the behavior experts say, although many owners can reel off accounts of cats urinating on shoes or other belongings of people who have irritated or neglected them. Such accounts are largely a matter of interpretation. Who can truly say what really goes on in a cat's mind?

Whatever the cause, house soiling is often symptomatic of emotional anxiety or physical discomfort. So whenever a cat begins eliminating in inappropriate places, consider urinary tract infections and other medical causes first. Take your cat to the veterinarian for a checkup. If the cause turns out to be physical, prompt medical treatment can reverse the problem before it becomes an established habit.

## Spraying vs. Urinating

If the urine stain appears to start primarily on a vertical surface—a wall or furniture leg—and drip down, the cat is spraying to mark territory. If the urine is pooled on a flat, horizontal surface—the floor or the bedcovers—the cat is squatting to eliminate urine. Ascertaining this difference is crucial because the factors that motivate each type of behavior are different. To effectively deal with either undesirable behavior, you must try to eliminate the factors that appear to be causing or influencing the situation.

There are some common motivating factors behind house-soiling problems:

**Location preference:** A cat that squats and inappropriately urinates on the carpet or floor may simply be expressing a dislike for the location of its litter box or for the texture of the litter. Perhaps the box is in a high foot-traffic area. Try moving the box to a quieter, more secluded part of the house, or if possible, place it at or near the site of the house-soiling "accident." For whatever reason, the cat may prefer that spot, and putting the box there may solve the problem.

**Litter preference:** If location doesn't seem to be a motivating factor, experiment with different types and textures of kitty litter. Some cats don't like litters treated with fancy perfumes and deodorizers and will refuse to use them. Some cats prefer fine-grained litter that is like sand, while others are content with the larger, coarser clay granules.

**Cleanliness:** In many cases, failure to use the litter box occurs because cat and owner have different opinions as to what constitutes a clean litter box. The owner may think cleaning the box once a week is enough, but the cat may want it cleaned every day. Cats are fastidious creatures, and digging in dirty, damp litter must be disgusting to them—perhaps a lot like being forced to use an unflushed toilet. So, if you're equally fastidious about removing the solid wastes daily and replacing soiled litter weekly, your cat likely will be more happily inclined to continue using the box without mishap.

**Anxiety:** Emotional causes of house soiling are the most difficult to pinpoint. Sometimes the sight of outdoor cats or the introduction of a new pet or a new baby into the household can trigger territorial spraying. In this situation, veterinarians can prescribe drugs that may ease the cat's anxiety and help suppress spraying and aggressive behaviors.

**Punishment:** Whatever the cause, punishing a cat for spraying or eliminating in inappropriate places is seldom effective and often makes matters worse. Rubbing your cat's nose in the mess will only make it fear you. Spanking the cat, then carrying it to the litter box may backfire and actually cause the animal to associate the abuse and fear with the litter box, an attitude that then becomes unnecessarily difficult to reverse. Rather than resort to punishment, identify and change the behavior by trial-and-error removal of any possible motivating factors, one by one, until you hit upon the right one and the problem resolves itself. Whenever you feel the situation isn't improving, seek the advice of an expert—your veterinarian or even an animal behavior consultant.

## Cleaning Up "Accidents"

To deter the cat from using the same spot as a toilet again, clean up house-soiling accidents with enzymatic products that dissolve the odor. Do this as quickly as possible; the more times your cat uses the same place, the more ingrained the bad habit will become. Several good odor-neutralizing products can be purchased at pet supply stores. A mix of white vinegar and warm water also works well. Avoid ammonia-based cleaners; ammonia is a urine by-product and might attract the cat back to the spot.

After you thoroughly clean the spot, make the surface less appealing to the cat by covering it temporarily with plastic, aluminum foil, sandpaper, window screen, or double-sided tape. If possible, keep the cat away from the area for a while.

# GROOMING YOUR MIXED BREED

## Grooming Supplies

Regular grooming is essential to control shedding and to keep your cat's coat looking nice. Brushing helps stimulate circulation and distribute natural oils through the coat, keeping the fur shiny and healthy looking. For a shorthaired cat, one 10-minute beauty session a week is usually sufficient, but if your cat has long hair, you will need to comb the coat daily to prevent matting. Regular combing helps remove the loose cat hairs from your cat's coat before they have a chance to shed off onto your furniture. To easily wipe cat hair off your furnishings, keep a brush, lint remover, or a damp cloth handy. Combing out loose hair is also the least expensive way to prevent hairballs.

To meet your cat's basic grooming needs, invest in pet or human nail clippers, several sizes of steel pet combs, and a natural-bristle brush. For kittens, start grooming with small and medium-size steel combs, and use a wide-toothed one on adult cats with plush, medium to long fur. For flea control, purchase a fine-toothed comb. Once caught in the comb's closely spaced teeth, fleas drown easily when dipped in a pan of water. A fine comb also readily removes flea dirt deep in the fur.

*Most cats learn to accept grooming, and many love the attention that they receive during their beauty sessions.*

The general condition of the coat is a good indicator of your cat's overall health. For instance, you'll want to schedule a visit to the veterinarian if you ever notice that your cat's skin is looking dry or flaky, or if the coat appears dull, looks oily, smells bad, or feels brittle. Several medical and dietary problems can affect the skin and hair coat, including allergies, parasites, and hormonal or nutritional imbalances, among others. By grooming regularly, you'll be much more likely to notice other problems, too, such as concealed cuts, scratches, lumps, or bumps that may warrant veterinary investigation, or even a hidden tick that has latched on for a blood meal.

## Shedding

Most people assume that the seasonal changes of hair coat are caused by temperature changes, but the experts say that environmental lighting primarily governs the shedding process. Under natural conditions, the lengthening sunlight hours in early spring trigger the cat's body to shed hair and grow a new coat in preparation for the changing season; similarly, autumn's shorter daylight hours cause the coat to thicken for winter. But when artificial, indoor lighting extends the daylight hours in the cat's environment, this natural cycle seems to get confused, resulting in a coat that sheds a little year-round.

# Grooming Routine

Most cats love the attention they get during grooming and learn to tolerate their beauty sessions readily. To get your cat accustomed to grooming, begin by spending a few minutes each day gently combing the fur with a metal comb. Once the cat is accustomed to the idea, you can space the sessions further apart.

On kittens, start with a small, fine-toothed comb, graduating to a medium- or wide-toothed comb as the cat matures, depending on how thick the coat is. For convenience and versatility, some combs come with closely spaced teeth on one end and wider-spaced teeth on the other end.

## Combing

Use the fine-toothed end of the comb on the shorter hair around the face, head, and chin. With the wide-space end, start at the base of the neck and gently comb the back and sides. Raise the chin a little to comb the throat and chest. When combing delicate areas, such as the belly, legs, and tail, be especially careful not to rake the comb's steel teeth against the sensitive skin. As you gently comb, remove any fur that may accumulate in the comb's teeth. Hair left in the comb tends to pull more hair out with it and may cause the cat some discomfort.

Establish a regular routine and grooming area—whether it's your lap or a countertop—and your cat will quickly learn what's expected when you place it in that spot and pick up the comb. Keep the sessions short, and don't forcibly restrain your cat if its attention wanders elsewhere.

During these sessions, get your cat accustomed to having its mouth gently opened, its ears touched, and its paws handled. This extra effort will pay off later when brushing teeth, administering medications, cleaning ears, and trimming claws (see page 62 for dental care tips). Make grooming sessions pleasant and always end with lots of praise and maybe even a special treat, and your cat will learn to eagerly anticipate the next one.

## Stripping the Longhaired Coat

During peak shedding periods, you may want to strip the coat of a longhaired cat occasionally by gently combing sections of fur against the way the hair lies. Called *back-combing*, this method removes the dead, loose hairs trapped closer to the skin as they are shed. To put the hair back in place, gently comb through it a second time, going the way the hair lies. Because overstripping can make the coat look flat and thin, you will want to comb *with* the lie of the hair most of the time, except when hair shedding is most noticeable.

## Brushing

If your cat seems to prefer brushing over combing, choose a soft, natural-bristle brush for the task. This will help reduce hair breakage and static. Always brush *with* the lie of the fur.

# Removing Mats

Mats are more common in longhaired cats, although shorthairs occasionally get them in their armpits or on their bellies and hind legs. When matting does occur, remove the unsightly hair clump right away, no matter how small. The longer a mat remains in the coat, the tighter it pulls the skin, causing discomfort to the cat. If neglected too long, mats

*When trimming claws, clip only the white tips. Avoid cutting into the pink "quick," as this will cause pain and bleeding.*

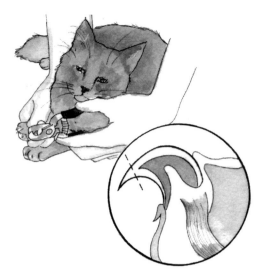

can irritate the skin severely enough to result in raw, open sores.

Inspect your cat's paws periodically for mats, too. Sometimes, tiny clumps of kitty litter or other debris can get stuck on the paw pads or between the toes and become especially painful. Mats in this area probably feel a lot like having a rock in your shoe.

To remove a mat, separate the tangle with your fingers and gently work it loose piece by piece, without yanking on the skin. To pick a stubborn mat loose, use the end teeth of a wide-toothed comb. If the mat is a massive clump, your last resort may be to clip it out with scissors or shave it off with electric trimmers, being careful not to cut the skin. Pet stores sell pet clippers and mat-splitters for such grooming problems.

## Trimming Claws

In addition to combing, toenail clipping is something you should get your cat accustomed to at a young age. Like your fingernails, cats' claws grow continuously and need to be clipped occasionally. Even with scratching posts available, an indoor cat's nails do not wear down as readily as an outdoor cat's. Neglected, untrimmed claws can curve under and grow back into the paw pads, causing a painful swelling and abscess. Trim claws once a month or so, and always prior to a cat show. Regular

trimming reduces the risk of injury to you and other family members and helps prevent snags in your carpets and furnishings.

Cats retract their claws when not in use. To extend them for trimming, hold the paw with your thumb on top and fingers on the bottom and gently squeeze. Before clipping, look closely at the nail and identify the *quick*. If the nail is white, the quick clearly shows up as a thin pink line running about three-fourths of the way down the nail toward the tip. To avoid cutting into the sensitive quick, trim the nail tip below the pink line. The quick contains nerves and blood vessels, but the nail tip below it does not. If you accidentally cut too high up into the pink quick, the cat will feel pain and the nail will bleed. If this happens, hold pressure over the wound with a cotton ball until the blood clots, or apply a shaving styptic. Don't forget the fifth claw slightly higher up on each inside forepaw.

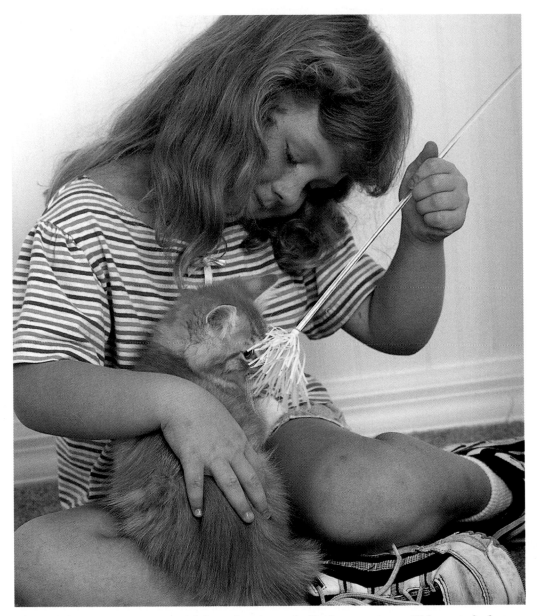

*If you end grooming sessions with lots of praise and affection, your cat will learn to look forward to them.*

*Cat grooming kit: soft and medium brushes, slicker brush, and comb.*

*Regular grooming helps keep your cat's coat clean and control the shedding of dead, loose hairs.*

*Use a fine-toothed comb on kittens and a medium- or wide-toothed comb on adults, depending on the thickness of their coat.*

# HOW–TO: BATHING

Generally, bathing your cat is only necessary when you are entering a cat show, or when the coat becomes flea-infested, excessively oily, or otherwise soiled enough to require a thorough cleaning. Too many baths can rob your cat's coat of natural oils and dry the skin.

### Pet Shampoos

Use only products labeled as SAFE FOR CATS. Never use dog shampoos or dog flea-control products on a cat, because the medication or flea insecticide in canine preparations may be too strong, even fatal, for cats. Also, not all cat flea products are safe for use on kittens, so read labels carefully before applying any shampoo, spray, dip, or powder to a kitten's fur. If the label doesn't specifically say that the product is safe for use on kittens, don't risk using

it. Ask your veterinarian to recommend a product.

### Other Supplies

For the bath, you'll also need:
- ✔ a comb
- ✔ cotton balls (for swabbing the ears)
- ✔ a blow-dryer
- ✔ towels
- ✔ a washcloth
- ✔ a sink or tub
- ✔ a pitcher or shower spray attachment
- ✔ a source of clean, warm water for washing and rinsing

The kitchen sink is usually the ideal place for the job, but if you must bathe the cat in a laundry tub, reserve a second tub of clean water for rinsing. For blow-drying the cat, you'll need a table or countertop with access to an electrical outlet. You'll probably also need a willing assis-

tant, because many cat baths easily turn into two-person productions, especially if the feline is not fond of or used to the idea.

### The Bath

Allow the cat to sit or stand in the basin and, if necessary, have your assistant gently hold the animal in place. Keep the cat's head *above* water at all times and turned away from the direction of the spray or faucet. Be especially careful not to splash or spray water in the cat's face.

Wet the fur first with warm, not hot, water, using the pitcher to dip and pour over the cat's back. If using a spray nozzle, keep the water pressure low to avoid frightening the cat. After wetting the fur sufficiently, apply shampoo and form a lather, starting at the neck and working back toward the tail. To lather the belly, have your assistant hold up the front legs. Avoid getting soap near the cat's face and eyes. Use a damp washcloth or moistened cotton balls to gently wet the head and wipe the face and eye areas clean.

### The Rinse Cycle

To remove all traces of shampoo, spend twice as much time rinsing as you do lathering. This is important because any residue left behind in the fur could make

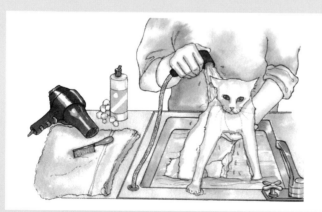

*When using a spray nozzle for bathing a cat, keep the water pressure low to avoid frightening the animal. Use warm water, not hot, and never spray the water directly in the cat's face.*

the coat look flat and greasy and cause itching and irritation. In some cases, the irritation may become so uncomfortable days later that the cat will actually scratch out portions of its fur, leaving behind ugly bald patches.

When the fur feels squeaky clean, drain off the water and gently press out the excess by running your hands down the back, legs, and tail. Lift the cat out of the tub or sink, being careful to support its rear end with one hand, and place it on a table or countertop for drying.

## Drying

Towel dry the sopping fur as much as possible first, then, follow up with a hand-held or stand-mounted blow-dryer to remove the remaining moisture. Like bathing, many cats will learn to tolerate blow-drying if you exercise some sensitivity when introducing them to the idea. Use only the low settings, never the hottest setting. And never blow air directly in the cat's face.

Gently comb the fur as you blow-dry, or separate the damp hair with your fingers, starting at the neck and working back toward the tail. Don't forget to dry the cat's underside. Have your assistant hold up the front legs for easier access to the belly and between the hind legs.

## Cleaning the Ears

Finally, use cotton balls to gently wipe away any dirt or wax visible just inside the ear flaps, but never poke cotton swabs or other objects into the ear canal, as this could cause injury to the delicate ear structures. If the ears show an excessive amount of dirty, crumbly, brown wax inside, or if they exude a fruity odor, have your veterinarian check for ear mites or fungal infections.

*When blow-drying, use only the lowest setting and avoid blowing air directly in the cat's face. You may need an assistant to hold the cat while you dry the underbelly.*

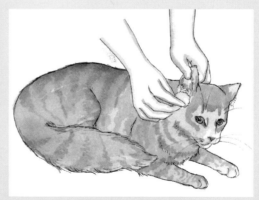

*Clean the ear flaps with a cotton ball, but never stick a cotton-tipped swab or other object into the ear canal.*

# SHOWING YOUR MIXED BREED

## Household Pet Competitions

Many people are surprised to learn that most major cat shows have classes for mixed-breed or non-pedigreed cats. Spectators at cat shows may admire the purebreds, but they readily recognize the household pets as being most similar to "Fluffy" at home. Show organizers hope that people will be encouraged to take better care of their pet cats when they see how beautifully presented and valued they are at a show.

Called the household pet (HHP) category, competition is open to non-pedigreed cats at least four months old. Household pets older than eight months must be spayed or neutered to compete. CFA and CFF do not permit declawed cats to be shown, but the other associations do not exclude or penalize HHPs for having had their claws removed. To further celebrate the value of all pets, TICA allows HHPs with physical handicaps, such as a missing leg or eye. TICA also has a general written standard for household pets.

HHPs can be of any size, color, or hair length. Depending on the association sponsoring the show, HHPs may be shown against other cats of the same color, or they may all be judged

*Unusual, attractive markings can catch the judge's eye and give mixed-breed cats an edge in the Household Pet division, where they are judged on personality, presentation, and beauty.*

together. HHPs are not judged according to a formal breed standard. Instead, they are judged on more general and subjective terms for their overall condition, beauty, personality, and show "presence."

Most HHPs are mixed breeds, but some are pet-quality purebreds that don't meet their breed's standard. Some cat-registering associations permit a purebred cat to be shown as a household pet, as long as the owner surrenders the papers or does not register the cat as a purebred.

## The Cat Show Setup

### Rings

The HHP category is a good place for novice exhibitors to learn how cat shows work. In the United States, the judging takes place on tables set up in one area of the show hall in full view of all spectators and exhibitors. Behind each judging table rests a row of cages, where cats entered in the same category are called to await their turn to be judged. This setup of tables and cages is called a judging ring.

A single exhibition may have four or more judging rings set up, each operating as a separate competition and presided over by a different judge. Sometimes, separate clubs present back-to-back shows consisting of eight to ten rings over a two-day weekend. Cats can compete in all rings for which they are eligible. Depending on the association sponsoring the show, various divisions and classes exist for eligible pedigreed cats, altered cats, kittens, household pets, and new or experimental breeds and colors. Not all shows have classes for household pets.

### Judging

In the ring, the judge removes each cat from its cage, places it on the judging table in view of the audience, and thoroughly examines it. After evaluating all cats in the ring, the judge awards ribbons to the winners. Pedigreed cats are judged according to how closely they meet the written standard of perfection for their breed, pattern, and color. Because not all associations have written standards for household pets, HHPs are judged by different criteria, based primarily on their overall health and demeanor.

### Awards

After achieving a specified number of wins, purebreds become champions and can compete against other champions for the coveted title of grand champion. HHPs also compete for comparable awards and titles, although the names differ from one association to another. In TICA, for example, household pets strive to win their "Masters," with the most coveted honor being Supreme Grand Master. In the AACE, HHPs progress in rank from Regal, to Imperial, to Superior Household Pet.

In some associations, points scored at each show accumulate toward year-end awards. The Happy Household Pet Cat Club (see page 92 for address) gives its members national, regional, and state awards every year based on a cat's

performance throughout the show season. To understand the ribbons, points, and awards system more fully, consult the cat club or association sponsoring the shows you enter.

## Entering a Cat Show

### Where to Start

First, find out about any upcoming purebred shows that are going to be held near you, as most will include a household pet division. Check listings in the cat fanciers' magazines, watch newspaper ads, or look for signs at pet stores and veterinarians' offices. The cat-registering associations listed in the back of this book also can provide information about affiliated cat shows and clubs in your area.

### Entry Forms

After you find a show to enter, contact the entry clerk for an entry form and ask about the rules. For example, if your cat is declawed or handicapped, make sure that it will be allowed in the show. You don't want to be disqualified on the day of the show simply because you didn't know the rules in advance.

After you receive the necessary forms, complete and return them with the appropriate fees. If you don't know how to fill in some of the blanks on the form, ask the entry clerk.

**Benching cages** for a single cat are small—usually about 2 feet wide by 2 feet high by 2 feet deep (61 cm × 61 cm × 61 cm), but for a little extra money, you may have the option of requesting a double cage on the entry form you submit. Your benching assignment is the cage where your cat will stay when it is not being judged in the ring.

## Show Supplies

Having submitted your entry, all you have to do now is get your cat ready and presentable for the show date. On the day of the show, you will need to bring some spray disinfectant to wipe down your cat's cage, plus fabric, towels, or show curtains to line the inside and bottom of the cage. Covering the cage gives your cat a little privacy amid the show hall noise and shields it from seeing the other cats in adjacent cages. This also adds an element of fun, because many shows have contests for the best-decorated cage.

Generally, the show committee provides a chair at each cage, cat litter, and sometimes disposable litter boxes. You'll have to bring a small litter pan, just in case, plus your grooming equipment, a grooming table (a sturdy TV tray or plastic patio table serve the same purpose), a cat carrier, a cat bed, food and water bowls, your cat's favorite food, and any other accessories to make your cat feel comfortable. It's also a good idea to take a gallon or two of water from home, or bottled water, because different drinking water can sometimes bring on diarrhea.

The show flyer should recommend hotels that allow pets. If not, ask in advance about the pet policy at the place where you plan to stay, and take a litter box for use in the hotel room.

### Preparations

Complete most of your cat's grooming at home a day or two before the show, so that only touch-ups should be required at the show. Clip the claws on all four feet and bathe the cat to make sure it has no sign of fleas or dirt in the coat. Make sure any shampoo you use is labeled as safe for cats. Remove any mats from the hair coat. Remember, a cat show is a beauty contest, and you want yours to look its best.

# The Day of the Show

When the big day arrives, transport the cat in its carrier. Check in early at the door and get your cat settled in its assigned cage. Read the catalog schedule to determine when your cat will be judged. Also, note the number for your entry in the catalog, as this is how your cat will be called to the ring. When you hear your cat's number called, carry your cat to the appropriate judging ring. Your number will be posted on top of one of the cages in the ring. Place your cat in the correct cage, then take a seat in the audience to watch the judging.

The judge will examine each cat in turn on the table and hang ribbons on the winners' cages at the end of the class. When the judging is over, the clerk will ask the exhibitors to remove their cats from the ring. Collect your cat and ribbons, if any, and return to your benching cage to await any further calls to the ring.

# A Responsible Attitude

Whether you show your cat or not, you have an opportunity to demonstrate to others how to properly care for a feline companion. Many cat owners take this responsibility seriously and strive to become educated pet owners. They visit shows, attend pet care seminars, participate in clubs, read books, and subscribe to cat magazines. Some even volunteer in their local humane shelters, helping to improve the plight and existence of all cats.

Such an attitude is admirable, because the cat or kitten you acquire represents a significant commitment on your part. The more strongly you communicate the value of this commitment to others, the more likely you are to instill a similar appreciation in others about cats.

# INFORMATION

## Cat Club

Happy Household Pet Cat Club
14508 Chester Avenue
Saratoga, CA 95070
(408) 872-0591
E-mail: banditzmom@fozztexx.com
Web page: http://www.best.com/~slewis/HHPCC/

## North American Cat Registries

American Association of Cat
   Enthusiasts (AACE)
P.O. Box 213
Pine Brook, NJ 07058
(973) 335-6717
Web page: http://www.aaceinc.org

American Cat Association (ACA)
8101 Katherine Avenue
Panorama City, CA 91402
(818) 781-5656

American Cat Fanciers Association (ACFA)
P.O. Box 203
Point Lookout, MO 65726
(417) 334-5430
Web page: http://www.acfacat.com

Canadian Cat Association (CCA)
220 Advance Boulevard, Suite 101
Brampton, Ontario L6T 4J5 Canada
(905) 459-1481
Web page: http://www.cca-afc.com

Cat Fanciers' Association (CFA)
1805 Atlantic Avenue
P.O. Box 1005
Manasquan, NJ 08736-0805
(732) 528-9797
Web page: http://www.cfainc.org

Cat Fanciers' Federation (CFF)
Box 661
Gratis, OH 45330
(937) 787-9009
Web page: http://www.cffinc.org

National Cat Fanciers' Association (NCFA)
10215 West Mount Morris Road
Flushing, MI 48433
(810) 659-9517

The International Cat Association (TICA)
P.O. Box 2684
Harlingen, TX 78551
(956) 428-8046
Web page: http://www.covesoft.com/tca/

United Feline Organization (UFO)
P.O. Box 3234
Lacey, WA 98509-3234
(360) 438-6903
Web page: http://ufo1nw@aol.com

## Noteworthy Organizations

Association of American Feed
   Control Officials, Inc. (AAFCO)
c/o Georgia Department of Agriculture
Agriculture Building, Capitol Square
Atlanta, GA 30334

National Animal Poison Control Center
University of Illinois College of Veterinary
   Medicine
2001 South Lincoln Avenue
Urbana, IL 61801
(800) 548-2423
(900) 680-0000
Note: Fee charged for crisis management

## Cat Publications

*CATS* Magazine
Subscriptions:
P.O. Box 56886
Boulder, CO 80322-6886
(800) 829-9125

Corporate offices:
2 News Plaza
P.O. Box 1790
Peoria, IL 61656
(309) 682-6626

*Cat Fancy*
Subscriptions:
P.O. Box 52864
Boulder, CO 80322-2864
(800) 365-4421

Editorial offices:
P.O. Box 6050
Mission Viejo, CA 92690
(949) 855-8822

*Cat Fancier's Almanac*
Cat Fanciers' Association
1805 Atlantic Avenue
P.O. Box 1005
Manasquan, NJ 08736-0805
(732) 528-9797

*CATsumer Report*
P.O. Box 10069
Austin, TX 78766-1069
(800) 968-1738

*Catnip* (newsletter)
Tufts University School of Veterinary Medicine
Subscriptions:
P.O. Box 420235
Palm Coast, FL 32142
(800) 829-0926

Editorial offices:
300 Atlantic Street, 10th Floor
Stamford, CT 06901
(203) 353-6650

*CatWatch* (newsletter)
Cornell University College of Veterinary Medicine
Subscriptions:
P.O. Box 420235
Palm Coast, FL 32142
(800) 829-8893

Editorial offices:
Torstar Publications, Inc.
99 Hawley Lane, Suite 1440
Stratford, CT 06497

## Books

Carlson, Delbert G., D.V.M., and James M. Giffin, M.D. *Cat Owner's Veterinary Handbook.* New York: Howell Book House, 1983.

Davis, Karen Leigh. *Fat Cat, Finicky Cat: A Pet Owner's Guide to Pet Food and Feline Nutrition.* Hauppauge, New York: Barron's Educational Series, Inc., 1997.

Helgren, J. Anne. *Encyclopedia of Cat Breeds: A Complete Guide to the Domestic Cats of North America.* Hauppauge, New York: Barron's Educational Series, Inc., 1997.

Robinson, Roy. *Genetics for Cat Breeders.* 3rd ed. Oxford, England: Pergamon Press, 1991.

Siegal, Mordecai, and Cornell University. *The Cornell Book of Cats.* New York: Villard Books, 1989.

Taylor, David. *The Ultimate Cat Book.* New York: Simon and Schuster, 1989.

———. *You & Your Cat: A Complete Guide to the Health, Care and Behavior of Cats.* New York: Alfred A. Knopf, 1986.

Whiteley, H. Ellen, D.V.M. *Understanding and Training Your Cat or Kitten.* New York: Crown Trade Paperbacks, 1994.

Wright, Michael, and Sally Walters, eds. *The Book of the Cat.* New York: Summit Books, 1980.

## About the Author

Karen Leigh Davis, a professional member of the Cat Writers' Association, has a background in journalism and business writing. She has written a pet care column and numerous feature articles on cats and other companion animals for national and regional magazines and newspapers. As a freelance writer with more than 15 years of experience, she has conducted extensive research on animal-related topics with veterinarians, breeders, and other experts. Davis comes from a cat-loving family and has a lifetime of experience living in the company of cats. She has bred and shown Persians and Himalayans, but she finds all felines, purebred or mixed, domestic or wild, irresistibly charming and beautiful. She lives in Roanoke, Virginia, with four Persian cats.

### Important Note

When you handle cats, you may sometimes get scratched or bitten. If this happens, have a doctor treat the injuries immediately.

Make sure your cat receives all the necessary shots and dewormings, otherwise serious danger to the animal and to human health may arise. A few diseases and parasites can be communicated to humans. If your cat shows any signs of illness, you should definitely consult a veterinarian. If you are worried about your own health, see your doctor and tell him or her that you have cats.

Some people have allergic reactions to cats. If you think you might be allergic, see your doctor before you get a cat.

It is possible for a cat to cause damage to someone else's property and even to cause accidents. For your own protection you should make sure your insurance covers such eventualities, and you should definitely have liability insurance.

## Photo Credits

All photos by Norvia Behling.

© Copyright 1999 by Karen Leigh Davis

All rights reserved.
No part of this book may be reproduced in any form, by photostat, microfilm, xerography, or any other means, or incorporated into any information retrieval system, electronic or mechanical, without the written permission of the copyright owner.

*All inquiries should be addressed to:*
Barron's Educational Series, Inc.
250 Wireless Boulevard
Hauppauge, NY 11788
http://www.barronseduc.com

*Library of Congress Catalog Card No. 99-15226*

International Standard Book No. 0-7641-0805-0

**Library of Congress Cataloging-in-Publication Data**
Davis, Karen Leigh, 1953–
    Mixed-breed cats : everything about purchase, care, nutrition, health care, behavior, and showing / Karen Leigh Davis.
        p.   cm. — (A Complete pet owner's manual)
        Includes bibliographical references (p.   ) and index.
        ISBN 0-7641-0805-0 (pbk.)
        1. Cats. I. Title. II. Series.
    SF442.D366      1999
    636.8'0887—dc21                                    99-15226
                                                              CIP

Printed in Hong Kong
9 8 7 6 5 4 3 2 1